Ralph Fletcher
Boy Writers
Reclaiming Their Voices

Stenhouse Publishers
Portland, Maine

Pembroke Publishers Limited
Markham, Ontario

Stenhouse Publishers
www.stenhouse.com

Pembroke Publishers Limited
www.pembrokepublishers.com

Credits
Page iv: From the musical composition "When I Was a Boy" by Dar Williams, copyright 1995 Burning Field Music. Used with permission. All Rights Reserved.
Page 154: "Foul Shot" by Edwin Hoey. Copyright Weekly Reader Corp. Reprinted with permission.
Page 170: From "For Every 100 Girls . . ." Postsecondary Education OPPORTUNITY website. Copyright Tom Mortenson. Used with permission.
Page 175: "The Follower" by Jack Gantos. Copyright 2005. Reprinted with permission.

Library of Congress Cataloging-in-Publication Data
Fletcher, Ralph J.
    Boy writers : reclaiming their voices / Ralph Fletcher.
        p. cm.
    Includes bibliographical references and index.
    ISBN-13: 978-1-57110-425-0 (alk. paper)
    ISBN-10: 1-57110-425-9 (alk. paper)
    1. English language—Composition and exercises—Study and teaching (Elementary) 2. Creative writing (Elementary education) 3. Boys—Education (Elementary) 4. Sex differences in education. I. Title.
LB1576.F4758 2006
372.62'3081—dc22   2006024168

Published in Canada by
Pembroke Publishers Limited
538 Hood Road
Markham, Ontario L3R 3K9

Cover design, interior design, and typesetting by Martha Drury
Cover illustration by Ben Allen
Manufactured in the United States of America on acid-free paper
12 11 10 09 08 07 06   9 8 7 6 5 4 3 2 1

For all teachers
who reach out to boy writers
and give them a seat at the table

I won't forget when Peter Pan
came to my house, took my hand,
I said I was a boy, I'm glad he didn't check . . .

I learned to fly, I learned to fight,
I lived a whole life in one night,
we saved each other's lives
out on the pirate's deck . . .

"When I Was a Boy" written and sung by Dar Williams

Contents

Acknowledgments

More than any book I have ever written, this one required assistance from many people. Without their thoughtful contributions, it never could have been written.

Tom Newkirk may not be a household name to teachers, but his books have had a profound influence on many writers today. Tom created the initial spark for this book when he wrote *Misreading Masculinity: Boys, Literacy, and Popular Culture*, a work that deeply impacted my thinking.

It was Franki Sibberson who suggested this book idea to me. She gave steady support and encouragement during all the months I wrote it. Thanks, Franki!

Special thanks go to Gayle and Max Brand, Gresham Brown, Matthew Debrocke, Jolene DiBrango, Betsy Dyches, Dana Goetz, Julie Leal, Darcy Maloney, Carolyn McKinney, and Robert A. Redmon. You guys were flat-out awesome. Early conversations with Don Graves, Stef Harvey, Don Murray, Katie Ray, Ladd Tobin, and Dan Fiegelson were very helpful in developing my thinking on this topic.

I am grateful to Carl Anderson, Doug Kaufman, Barry Lane, Peter H. Johnston, Isoke Nia, and Cyrene Wells for the ideas they contributed to this book.

Mega-thanks must go to Jennifer Allen and the members of the Boys Writing Club at Albert S. Hall School in Waterville, Maine. Jen was amazingly generous with her time and careful response to the drafts I wrote.

Artie Voigt, my friend/colleague/life coach, has a way of cutting to the heart of the matter; his wisdom infuses this book. Steve Tullar, Pete Schiat, and John Silverio are fine teachers in my local school district—their spirits live in this book. Thanks to Mary Baldwin, Carmen Barnhart, Lois Bridges, Melanie Crider, Mary Ellen Giacobbe, Martha Horn, Ellin Keene, Medea McEvoy, and Shelley Harwayne. Jack Gantos generously gave permission for me to include his story "The Follower" in this book. Thanks to Dar Williams for giving permission to reprint her song lyrics.

I am indebted to the many teachers who found time in their hectic lives to answer my survey questions. Their insights strengthen this book and give it a dimension I never could have provided on my own. These teachers include Aimee Buckner, Lori Collins, Valerie Collins, Ann Marie Corgill, Adam Crawley, Jill Crossley, Karen Durica, Kathleen Fay, Cindy Flegenheimer, Steve Freifeld, Todd Frimoth, Susie Garber, Jan Gilbert, Anne Hankins, Lisa Hansen, Lynn Herschlein, Vanessa Hill, Jody Kawamata-Chang, Doug Lambe, Dave Lantz, Lori Lefkowitz, Dean Looney, Lisa Lynch, Holly Martocci, Mike McCormick, Catherine Mergner, Andrea Morgan, Bruce Morgan, Steve Morse, Marianne Norman, Dennise O'Grady, Tess Pardini, Heather Perry, Carrie Pomeroy, Linda Rief, Michele Sodergren, Mary Lou Soloway, Kathy Spryou, Lisa Schwartzburg, Stuart Turner, Lori Ulewicz, Susannah Voigt, and Suzanne Whaley.

I also appreciate all the teachers who helped me survey the boys in their classes. In addition to the teachers already mentioned I wish to extend my sincere thanks to Jean G. Browne, Alice Cherniske, Erin Clendenen, Trish Epifanio, Jan Furuta, Judy Gardner, Alison Hamilton, Kathy Helmer, Dave Hoh, Melanie Rick, Dave Rynerson, Kathy Starosciak, and JoAnn Wong-Kam.

A huge thanks goes to Sam Zarfos, a fifth grader, whose interview appears in this book. Sam's passion and honesty were inspirational to me. Thanks also to Ben Allen, who generously provided artwork and writing samples.

Thank you to the boys who filled out my survey, including Santiago Cursi, Max Vojcsik, and Isaiah and Kadeem Wilcox. Thanks also to all the boys whose writing appears in this book, including Nicholas Van Nest, Ryan Thomas Bailey, Mark Serbent, Keenan

Williams, Jimmy Owens, Paulus Abuakel, Ryan Braley, Chris Minafo, Andres Vazquez, Aaron Tyson, Tyler Reeves, Alden Quimby, Oliver Leckenby, Matt Valley, Carter White, Thomas Sturtevant, and Joseph Fletcher.

Deep-root thanks go to my sons, Taylor, Adam, Robert, and Joseph. Watching them grow from baby boys to young men has been the best possible preparation for writing a book like this. Robert read piles of student writing samples and helped me identify ones I wanted to use for this book. His perspective as a teenage boy was invaluable.

Thanks to my five brothers, too: Jimmy, Tom, Bobby, John, and Joe. We grew up as boys together. And thanks to my father: his example gave me an image of what it means to be a man.

I appreciate Larry Swartz for taking the time to give this book a thorough reading early enough so I could use his ideas to strengthen the book.

Stenhouse editors Brenda Power, Philippa Stratton, and Bill Varner helped me bring this book into focus. Philippa cleared her mental decks for this project, immersed herself in literature around boys' literacy, and pushed me to write a far better book than I could have written on my own.

As for JoAnn Portalupi, what can I say about someone who is my wife, frequent coauthor, and best friend? I appreciate her professional wisdom (she helped me nail down the subtitle), but I am most grateful to her for being such a wonderful mother and helping our sons become strong, confident, tender men. I have seen it with my own eyes, JoAnn: they grow toward your light.

Skiing
Nicholas Van Nest, Grade 6

Icy frost whips against my goggles, the wind, tearing through my clothes. My skis feeling as if they're on fire as I speed down the hill toward the stunt ramp. Suddenly I flash back to last year's vacation when I had been in the same boots racing down this very hill. I had forgotten to lean back, lost both skis from the ramp, and done a flip resulting in a head-plant. Well, that wasn't going to happen this year, I thought, as I gripped the ski poles tighter and leaned forward. The wind was screaming in my ears as if even the elements were cheering me on. Tilting backwards I pushed one last time, and let speed decide my fate. On to the ramp I flew, shooting into the air losing all sense of gravity, time, or space, just begging to pull through. SWOOSH! I felt vibrations tingling the bottom of my skis. I'd made it!

"I'm alive! Oh-ya!" I screamed. "In all of ya'll faces. You all disgraces. Pick up the paces."

In the snow, dancing in my skis, I realized a German couple was staring at me wide-eyed, and I heard the husband say: "Iz ziz how all crazy Americans act?"

RF   *A nifty slice-of-life story, full of action, wry humor, and triumph. Nicholas does a nice job of slowing down the hot spot; we really get inside the head of the narrator. I like how, at the end, he switches from his own point of view to the point of view of the tourists observing him.*

Chapter 1

The Trouble with Boys

Many boys have never seen writing as a viable option for them. Some are not "good students" in the traditional sense, so teachers figured if they produced anything it was a miracle . . . Many of these boys get teachers who instead of seeing the inherent good in a piece of writing see only the deficits and ways to make it "better" . . . For the boys, every assigned piece can be a nightmare because it is never good enough. The road is too long so they give up before they even start.

Fourth-grade literacy teacher

There was a problem. I didn't recognize it at first, although for years I had the vague sense that something was wrong when I spent time in writing workshops at various schools across the United States. I couldn't quite bring the issue into focus, too caught up in my role as a coach charged with helping teachers get the mechanics of the workshop (mini-lesson, conferences, classroom management, etc.) working properly. It's hard to be much of a researcher when you're usually brought into schools as an advocate for a particular way of teaching writing.

Still, it was there. It was like noticing something out of the corner of your eye; you're too focused on what's happening in front of you to bring total attention to events at the periphery of your vision.

If pressed to explain further I would describe a certain lack of energy, a spiritless, ho-hum, *do-we-really-have-to-do-this?* attitude I perceived in some of the classrooms. Maybe I was naïve, but it surprised me to find such lethargy in an active, hands-on structure like the writing workshop.

My breakthrough in understanding came a few years ago when I stumbled onto Tom Newkirk's book *Misreading Masculinity: Boys, Literacy, and Popular Culture* (2002). In his book Newkirk draws upon various pools of knowledge to construct a critique that I found both fascinating and devastating. Newkirk argues that we don't really understand the boys in our classrooms. We misunderstand their crude humor. Especially after the tragic shootings at Columbine High School, we fear their apparent thirst for violence, which is reflected in what they choose to read and write. Instead of trying to understand these boys we treat them as a problem to be managed. *Misreading Masculinity* rocked my world and would not allow me to return to my old way of seeing it.

I care a great deal about young writers and the teachers who work hard to nourish them. I have staked my professional reputation on the power of the writer's workshop. If there's a better structure for helping students learn to write, well, I'd like to see it. For twenty years I have worked as a consultant in classrooms across the country, helping teachers fine-tune their writing workshops. After reading *Misreading Masculinity* I turned my eyes toward the boys in those workshops, watching as they leaned forward to write poems, reports, narratives, persuasive essays.

Something seemed . . . off.

In any group of students you'll find a range of affect, ability, and attitude. In general, you find boys at the extremes—their ability range tends to be wider than the range for girls. In writing classrooms the same thing seemed to hold true. I noticed boy writers who were very enthusiastic and accomplished; I also noticed those who were resistant or disruptive. A few of the guys were writing with gusto, but the general demeanor of those boys troubled me. The boys seemed:

Turned off.
Checked out.
Disengaged.
Disenfranchised.

I observed most boys dutifully putting pencil to the paper, but many seemed to be merely going through the motions. Their scrunched-up body language was painful to see.

When I started interviewing boys, in person and through written surveys, I was struck by the pervasive lack of enthusiasm they showed for writing in school. Again, there was a wide range, but many boys told me they disliked writing; a few admitted that they despised it. Some of their comments reflected a sad realism about the mismatch between boys and school. Matt, a fifth grader, put it like this: "Boys want to just get the writing done fast so they can go outside and play sports."

It was disheartening to hear that these boys viewed writing as just another boring subject to be endured until you could finally get to the fun stuff. I found it even more dismaying when I realized that most of those boys were writing in a workshop setting. To me, the writing workshop resembles an industrial arts or gym class, a dynamic structure that celebrates choice and puts a premium on action. The workshop values learning by *doing* as opposed to talking about it, and is the very definition of constructivism in practice. As basketball announcer Dick Vitale might put it: "This is hands-on action, baby!" The writing workshop would seem to be a perfect arena for boys, tailor-made to their eclectic interests and boisterous energy.

What went wrong? (And why had it taken me so long to notice?) Boy writers were floundering; at least they seemed to be. I needed a reality check, and started talking with teachers around the country. My conversations and interviews confirmed my initial perception.

"I see a night-and-day difference between boy and girl writers," says Bruce Morgan, a fourth-grade teacher in Colorado and author of *Writing Through the Tween Years: Supporting Writers, Grades 3–6.* "As a rule, the boys do not like writing as much as the girls. Even with all the things I do to entice boys to write and bring their interests into the classroom, they still would avoid writing if they had the choice. I do writing in various genres to hopefully engage my male writers and that seems to help. But I still struggle on a daily basis to get the same quality from them that I get from the girls."

I created a written questionnaire designed to uncover teachers' perceptions of the boy writers with whom they work. I sent these surveys to roughly one hundred teachers around the United States and abroad and received seventy-one responses. Although seventy-one responses certainly does not represent a scientific sampling, I want to emphasize that these teachers were handpicked because I consider them to be among the strongest writing teachers around. These are individuals conversant with current theory who run a writer's workshop and work hard to motivate their boys. In the questionnaire I asked them to complete this sentence: "In general my (boys/girls) tend to enjoy writing more." The results are striking:

Girls: 49   Boys: 1   Both (equal): 21

My gut feeling tells me that these results would be skewed even more sharply in favor of the girls if you looked at a larger sampling of writing teachers. As you'll see in the next chapter, empirical data supports the idea that boy writers are struggling in relation to girl writers.

Widening the Circle

Newkirk ends *Misreading Masculinity* with a chapter titled "A Big Enough Room," in which he argues that we need to "widen the circle" when it comes to boys' reading and writing in schools. At this point I saw an opening. Rather than a broad look at boys' literacy, I wanted to write a book that would focus on boys' writing. Rather than looking only at the *why* I wanted to move to the *what*, and suggest practical ways we can widen the circle for our boy writers.

Writing teachers draw on three distinct pools of knowledge:

✖ What we know about teaching
✖ What we know about our students
✖ What we know about the craft of writing itself.

Most readers would associate me primarily with the third pool of knowledge—craft lessons, qualities of writing, and so forth. In this book I concentrate on the first two arenas, and suggest realistic ways we might create writing classrooms that are friendlier to our boys.

Revision is more than a strategy used in the writing process; it's also a metaphor for personal and professional growth. There comes a time when every reflective practitioner needs to step back, take an honest look at what is and is not working, and revise his or her teaching accordingly. Cultured pearls start when a bit of grit gets inserted into the oyster; I'm happy to be that grit.

Maureen Barbieri wrote a fine book, *Sounds from the Heart: Learning to Listen to Girls.* I once attended a workshop she gave on this topic. Halfway through the workshop a teacher raised her hand and angrily confronted Maureen.

"You're saying all this stuff about the girls, but what about the boys?" the woman demanded. "Don't the boys matter?"

"Of course they do!" Maureen smiled patiently. "All I'm saying here is that girls are important, and they've got unique issues. They deserve our attention. Give me one hour to talk about the girls. That's all I ask."

This exchange suggests the strong tendency to polarize in our culture, pitting one group against the other.

"Many times a week, a reporter or other media person will ask me: 'Why should we care so much about boys when men still run everything?'" says Michael Gurian (2005a, p. B1), author of *The Minds of Boys: Saving Our Sons from Falling Behind in School and Life* (2005b).

Tom Newkirk makes a similar point in *Misreading Masculinity.* "The focus on 'gaps' tends to pit boys against the girls, to emphasize either/or," he points out. "Yet surely it is possible to emphasize boys' difficulty in school without rejecting claims that girls may experience difficulties or inequities" (2002, p. 20).

Amen. I don't want to pull attention or yank funding away from the girls. The very last thing I want to do is to push the girls down in order to pull the boys up. But boy writers have unique strengths, quirks, and weaknesses that every thoughtful practitioner or parent will want to be aware of. What I want is only a slight variation of what Maureen Barbieri requested when I attended her workshop: Give me one book to talk about the boys.

I wanted this book to have a boy flavor; to that end I have inserted one boy writing sample between each chapter. Some teachers will find it difficult to embrace boy writing in all its grit and glory. The writing samples have been included to make the various ideas put forth in this book as concrete and tangible as possible. I hope these pieces will have a practical use in the classroom. I urge teachers to use them, in whole or in part, to model craft elements and to give students an image of strong boy writing.

Appendix E includes a story, "The Follower," written by Jack Gantos for *Guys Write for Guys Read* (Scieszka 2005). If boy writing is a genre unto itself, then "The Follower" is a classic example. As a father of boys this story alarmed me when I read it; as a guy myself it made me laugh out loud a half dozen times. Whether you find it funny or outrageous will depend upon your perspective.

Boy Writers is a piece of persuasive writing. I aim to convince you that although every boy writer is unique, as a group boys possess particular strengths and weaknesses. I'm well aware that any book that explores distinctions along gender lines will provide excellent fodder for intense discussion and even argument.

Nevertheless, the thrust of this book is practical, not political. To that end you'll find a section at the end of most chapters titled "What Can I Do in My Classroom?" where I make specific recommendations for ways you might rethink and revise classroom practice. I don't expect readers to agree with every suggestion offered in this book, but I hope it might serve as a catalyst for teachers to think deeply about what concrete steps we can take to do a better job of teaching boys to write.

We must begin by coming to grips with the qualities boys bring to the table. To the extent that we really understand them we can become more skilled, more complete writing teachers.

Beach Trap

Ryan Thomas Bailey

First,
Get a one-gallon milk jug
With a cap that can pop off
Fill it with ocean water
Ease the cap on
Just barely
Bury it
Remind yourself
Not to step on it

The beach
Suddenly becomes
A minefield

While you're waiting
For an unsuspecting passerby
Pull up a chair
Go swimming
Dig a hole
Fly a kite
Annoy your brother
Go inner tubing
Or boogie boarding
Or even fishing
Wait, someone's coming!

 Why is it that boys universally love to concoct secret traps to snare the bad guys? Some might raise their eyebrows at the idea of turning a peaceful beach into a minefield, but I find it wonderfully imaginative. I admire the sly, playful tone. Great ending—leaves us at a moment of high suspense.

Chapter 2

Failure to Thrive

Picture a student in your class who is really struggling with reading and writing. This student doesn't like to read, has difficulty sitting still and paying attention, and turns in crumpled, half-completed homework. We've all had students like this. But chances are, as you picture this child in your mind, you are thinking of one of the boys in your class.

Diane Connell and Betsy Gunzelmann, "The New Gender Gap"

In the field of pediatrics there is a syndrome known as "failure to thrive." Basically, the baby stops gaining weight and growing developmentally the way a healthy baby should. This syndrome can be described in numerical terms: lack of weight gain versus normal weight gain, percentiles and growth charts, and so forth. This statistical information, however important, doesn't begin to express the true anguish of panicking parents as they watch their struggling infant.

A similar thing is true for boy writers. The data on boys' writing achievement is alarming, but it tells only part of the story. Let's take a quick look at the statistics before going into the classrooms to meet writing teachers and the boys they teach.

In writing this book I looked at a blizzard of statistics and test scores in a rather haphazard sequence. The first sobering data I found appeared in a newspaper article that examined national trends in the percentage of young men and young women in college. In the 1960s through the mid-1970s, the college student population stood roughly fifty-fifty—half men, half women. Since that time the college population has been steadily trending toward more women, fewer men. In 2005, the national college population broke down to 57 percent female, 43 percent male.

"Not only do national statistics forecast a continued decline in the percentage of males on college campuses, but the drops are seen in all races, income groups and fields of study," says policy analyst Thomas Mortenson, publisher of the influential *Postsecondary Education Opportunity* newsletter in Oskaloosa, Iowa. Since 1995 he has been tracking—and sounding the alarm about—the dwindling presence of men in colleges. Of course, you can't wholly attribute this alarming trend to boys' weakness in writing ability; still, the 57/43 split is an eye-opener. (I live in the Seacoast of New Hampshire. There are twelve high schools in the area; in 2006 only one had a boy valedictorian. In each of the high schools the top ten students were mostly girls.)

Next I looked at the data on writing achievement. I was particularly interested in the difference between boys' and girls' test scores. I looked first at the state of Washington. Here is the latest data available, for the years 2004–2005. The graph in Figure 2–1 shows the percentage of students "meeting the standard" on the state writing test.

As you can see, there's an 18-plus percentage difference between girls' and boys' scores, an achievement gap that continues throughout the grades. When I looked at other states I found the same thing—girls trouncing boys on state writing tests. It turns out that the achievement gap in writing is not isolated to a few states but is a national phenomenon. The National Assessment of Educational Progress (NAEP) writing tests in July 2003 showed boys scoring an average of 24 points lower than girls (see National Center for Education Statistics [NCES] data, Appendix A).

Every bit of hard data I have seen shows boys scoring significantly lower than their female counterparts on writing tests. Don't take my word for it; go to your state's department of education website. Look at test scores for writing tests, and see if they provide results that are broken out by gender. It's true that writing tests are not the only measure of writing ability, but surely the difference between boys' and girls' test scores should send up a warning flare.

	Boys	Girls	Difference
Fourth grade	48.6	67.3	18.7
Seventh grade	52.2	70.9	18.7
Tenth grade	56.3	74.9	18.6

Source: Office of Superintendent of Public Instruction. Washington State Report Card, 2004–2005.
http://reportcard.ospi.K12.wa.us.

FIGURE 2–1 PERCENTAGE OF STUDENTS MEETING THE STANDARD ON WASHINGTON STATE WRITING ASSESSMENT, 2004–2005.

The gap between boys' achievement in writing and girls' achievement in writing is disturbing. I wondered: do teachers observe the same thing in the classroom? In my teacher survey I asked about that. With very few exceptions, the teachers perceived a discrepancy that favored girls.

"My weakest writers (or my refusers, really, who won't write, even if it means they fail my class or barely pass) almost always tend to be boys," reported Susannah Voigt, high school English teacher in Brooklyn.

"The girls like the way writing captures their voices," said Linda Rief, a seventh- and eighth-grade language arts teacher and author of several professional books. "They enjoy seeing their words on paper. They are more patient with feedback and willing to take the time to polish a piece of writing. Boys tend to want immediate feedback and hope the reader just likes the writing the way it is. (I got my point across, it fulfilled the assignment, let's move on.)"

"I think that girls are encouraged to express themselves from a very young age so writing tends to come more naturally for many of them," suggested Carrie Pomeroy, a fifth-grade teacher in Alabama. "Girls tend to 'attack' a writing assignment and get it done quickly. Boys, on the other hand, tend to ponder and fester about what they are going to write."

Darcy Maloney, an English teacher in Louisville, Kentucky, summed up the difference like this: "My girls are more prolific, entering into most new projects, assignments, and writer's notebook work comfortably. The girls don't shy away from the emotional component of poetry. My boys are slower starters, less verbose and prolific, and prefer to employ humor whenever possible."

At the end of my written survey I asked teachers to complete this sentence: "What perplexes me about my boy writers is . . ." Here are some of their responses.

"The resistance to write and then the lack of perseverance," replied Lori Ulewicz, a fourth-grade teacher in Troy, Michigan.

"Why they don't want to get started writing," said Anne Hankins, fifth-grade teacher at the Beijing International School in China. "They love to talk about events in their lives, but not to put it on paper."

"They [boys] have such powerful feelings about the world and everything that happens in it and to them," noted Isoke Nia, "but it's so *not a cool thing* to let us [adults] or them [other boys] or them [other girls] know it. They try to avoid the core, and their writing only scratches the surface much too often."

Teachers' perceptions and careful observations help humanize the numbers, and shed important light on this issue. Even so, the issue feels abstract until you start thinking in terms of actual boys and their experiences expressing themselves through written words.

I remember that my son Robert wrote a story titled the "Rainbow-Headed People" when he was in first grade. It was one of his first stories, a tale with fabulous illustrations that made me smile every time I read it.

I remember two boys I worked with, Troy and Miguel, who wrote a poem titled "Girls" that began with a line that has stuck with me all these years: "Girls, girls, with finicky hair . . ."

I watched Max and Brendan, third graders, collaborate on a book about evil animals, which they titled "When Good Animals Go Bad."

I remember all the stories, poems, letters, reports, thank-you notes, and college entrance essays, written by my four sons.

The Russian submarine *Kursk* sank in August 2000. The world watched in horror as the oxygen slowly ran out, and all the men died. One of the officers on board the sub, Dmitry Kolesnikov, wrote about the plight of himself and the men under his command: "All the crew from the sixth, seventh, and eighth compartments went over to the ninth. There are 23 people here. We made this decision as a result of the accident. None of us can get to the surface."

When the electrical battery failed, and the lights went out, Kolesnikov wrote: "I am writing blind."

This heartbreaking story is a reminder that writing is much more than just another school subject. It is a life skill, a lifeline we throw out at the darkest, as well as the most triumphant, moments of our lives. Alas, I think too many boys today feel as if they are "writing blind."

"Failure to thrive" is a phrase that reminds me of boys I see in writing classrooms. As a group they may not be failing miserably, but can we honestly say that they are thriving? These boys need our patience, encouragement, and most intelligent support. Pediatricians take "failure to thrive" syndrome very seriously—and so should we. We simply cannot afford to write off a generation of boy writers. Writing is a skill that no student, no citizen, can do without.

Bettaie

Mark Serbent, Grade 5

I would like to write about my pet Beta fish. His name is Bettaie (Bait-e). More specifically when I got Bettaie. One lead may sound like:

One marvelous day at the Waterville Wal-Mart a 10 year old boy named Mark would get a friend he could talk to about anything but would reply nothing more than a blub. !Blub!

One magnificent marvelous day at the Waterville Wal-Mart a 10 year old boy named Mark would get a friend he would talk to for hours and he would not reply with anything more than a "blub!" One enthusiastic "BLUB!"

Okay, it started in early September. I just moved to Maine from upstate New York. I just started a new school and you guessed it I just wanted 1 friend, just one friend I could always talk to and I knew was always there. So one day my Mom took us out to eat and said we could go to Wal-Mart and get something under 20 bucks. I immediately knew what I wanted. I wanted a pet Beta.

When we got to Wal-Mart my sister said: "Let's go to electronics!" Todd hollored: "No, let's go to toys!" I said okay and after what seemed like waiting forever (I have little to no patience) my Mom asked me where I wanted to go. I replied: "Um . . . I think it's under pets." Mom said: "Only one fish." I was perfectly fine with that. After all you only make 1 friend at a time.

When we got to where the fish were I picked out a home first. I knew I wanted to get home once I picked my Beta out. I looked long and hard to find which fish I liked but I guess Mom was right. You can't go searching for a friend, you have to let your friend come to you. Sure enough one red and blue fish swam up and looked at me. I knew this would be the beginning of an awkward friendship.

Once I got home I had to get the fish in his tank and most importantly name him. After one hour I gave up. Bettaie. That's it. Perfect. I don't mean it as bait but Bettaie as in Beta. Then it was time for bed. No gloating about a brilliant name tonight.

Now it is a not so magnificent-marvelous day in March. It's bitterly cold and I'm cooped up inside and you guessed it, I've got a fish to cheer me up.

 This is a piece of "meta-fiction" in the sense that Mark lets the reader see him trying to construct the right lead. The story contains a number of wisecracking asides but, at the same time, it's a very tender piece. One thing I admire about Mark's story is how he starts by talking about friendship and weaves that theme throughout the piece until the very end.

Chapter 3

The Gender Filter

In general my girls like writing better than my boys. I believe that our culture teaches that men are to be strong and, somehow, writing is seen as a "girl" thing and for soft young men.

Isoke Nia, literacy consultant

The Exceptions

Friends of mine, brave souls indeed, hosted a sixth-grade boy/girl party. At one point, fifteen kids were crammed into the den playing video games. What would be your guess about the gender of those kids playing video games? Girls? Boys? A mix of the two?

This is a no-brainer: boys. A few girls wandered over for a few minutes, checked out the scene, then left. Boys, as every parent knows, almost universally adore video games. But that does not mean that *all* the boys at the party spent their time in front of the X-Box. In fact, two boys sat out on the porch, hammering the chips and dip, chatting up the girls. Another boy raced around the house, chasing an energetic German shepherd.

In the same way, I would argue that when you talk about boy writers you will find recognizable characteristics that are pretty consistent within this group. But exceptions certainly do exist. Some boys are drawn to writing at an early age, and absolutely love it. Heck, I'm an exception myself. As a student I was a sit-down, shut-up, listen-to-the-teacher, follow-the-rules kind of kid. I could play the game called School as well as any of the girls. Today I write books that usually contain more emotion and introspection than action and violence. My boys were dismayed when my first published book for young readers turned out to be a collection of love poems.

"Why did you have to write a book about love poems?" my ten-year-old son, Adam, asked glumly when it came out.

Still, despite the exceptions, boy writers do reveal a pattern of strengths, weaknesses, and quirky behavior. But first and foremost boys are individuals. Any new understandings we develop in this area should be used to open new possibilities for boy writers, not restrict them.

Gender is an explosive subject. While I was working on this book, I got a phone call from a friend, a woman who also happens to work in the field of literacy education. I hadn't spoken to her in ages, and it felt good to finally get the chance to catch up. I mentioned this book about boys' writing, and shared with her some of the alarming statistical data I'd been looking at.

"That's not accurate," she interrupted. "The gap closes by the time kids hit high school."

"That's not true," I replied. "I—"

"It is true," she insisted.

"Did you read the *Newsweek* article?" I shot back. "Twelfth-grade girls score 24 percent higher than boys on standardized writing tests. I've got it right here."

"It's a waste of time to look at gross data like that," she said. "It's completely misleading. You've got to break out the numbers by race and class."

Amazing: I hadn't talked to my friend once in eight months. Yet here we were, ten minutes into the phone call, already arguing with each other! The trigger? Gender. During our heated exchange my friend seemed uninterested in what I'd been learning on this subject. She pressed her point of view, minimizing the gap between boy and girl writers. And perhaps I, who had taken up the cause of boy writers for this book, had my own ax to grind. Anyway, the argument ended with a hasty good-bye and halfhearted promise to "get together soon." (We haven't.)

If life has taught me anything it is that people's opinions/feelings about gender run deep and can be inscrutable, even irrational. Our ideas/images/values connected to what it means to be a man or a woman are deeply entrenched, lurking in some primitive part of our brains. Gender is a thick stew, with sex, biology, popular culture, and power bubbling just beneath its hot surface. And now literacy. No wonder conversations about gender are so explosive. No wonder there have been so many books and articles arguing for and against the fact that boys are getting shortchanged in U.S. schools.

"Girl behavior becomes the gold standard [in school]," says Michael Thompson, coauthor of *Raising Cain*, a widely read book and PBS TV special. "Boys are treated like defective girls" (Tyre 2006, p. 48).

"Now we're seeing what's wrong with the system for millions of boys," says Michael Gurian, author of another best seller, *The Minds of Boys: Saving Our Sons from Falling Behind in School and Life*. "Beginning in very early grades, the sit-still, read-your-book, raise-your-hand-quietly, don't-learn-by-doing-but-by-taking-notes classroom is a worse fit for more boys than it is for most girls." Gurian adds: "Boys have a lot of Huck Finn in them—they don't, on average, learn as well as girls by sitting still, concentrating, multi-tasking, listening to words" (2005a, p. B1).

Thirty years ago differences between boys and girls were largely explained by the different ways the sexes are socialized—in other words, the influence of culture. Today it's becoming clear that there are innate differences between boys and girls, including anatomical differences in the brain. In females the corpus collosum (the part that connects the two hemispheres of the brain and allows them to communicate with each other) is about 20 percent larger than it is in males.

Some of these differences have made their way into pop culture, and there's a certain amount of misinformation that gets passed off as gospel truth. But many differences between the sexes *are* real, and have been confirmed by research studies. Boys do tend to have better hand-eye coordination than girls, for example, but have weaker fine-motor coordination (as we'll see in Chapter 9). Baby girls have better hearing than do baby boys.

How do we make sense of all this? Let's start by acknowledging that it's very difficult to be completely neutral in this discussion because we are all gendered beings, born with either XX or XY chromosomes. Furthermore, our beliefs in this area are sculpted by our personal history as a female or a male. Gender is not like a mask you can take off and put aside for a few hours; it is an inherent part of who we are. We each have a "gender filter" that can enhance but also distort our perceptions of the world. This filter can be as powerful as the filters we have for race or class.

This gender filter works in several ways. Having a "boy filter" affects how boys perceive school. It also colors how they perceive themselves as writers. Shelley Peterson (2000), a professor at the Ontario Institute for Studies in Education at the University of Toronto, asked students in Ohio to analyze writing samples from neighboring school districts. Four hundred students were given nine student writing samples and were asked to identify the author's gender for each sample. Peterson's study found that students guessed the author was female when the stories were descriptive and well written, and guessed the author was male when the stories contained spelling errors and poor grammar.

Also according to Peterson's study, female students wrote more about relationships and emotions in their stories, and males wrote more about violence and action. In an interview with Sue Toye (2000), Peterson explained, "If boys did write about relationships, their peers used disparaging remarks to critique their stories." If this study is accurate it suggests boys' gender does influence the way boys perceive themselves as writers, and the perception isn't a positive one.

What about us? Does *our* gender color the way we perceive boy writers? Ninety percent of elementary school teachers are women. Would it be shocking to learn that teachers tend to create classrooms that favor the tastes, strengths, sensibilities, and learning styles of girls?

In my survey, I asked teachers to reflect on what impact or effect they believe their gender has, if any, on how they teach writing. I asked, "Although we like to think of ourselves as responding equally to both boys and girls, in fact we may tend to favor one gender over another. To which gender, if any, do you think you tend to respond more favorably? Why?"

Roughly half the teachers who responded described themselves as truly "sex-blind" and believed they responded equally to girl and boy writers. Perhaps they do. Here are some responses from those teachers who admitted a preference for working with their boy or girl writers.

"Girls—probably because I went to an all-girls high school," replied Mary Lou Soloway, a literacy coach in Virginia. "I'm always rooting for the girls and pushing them along more, telling them they can do it. Most teachers respond more to the boys (by middle and high school it will only get worse) and I make a point to do the opposite."

"Definitely boys," Bruce Morgan said. "I always want the hard kids, the ones who have been turned off by school and feel like failures. That is my favorite kid. Give me your tired, your poor, your huddled masses yearning to be the hell away from school. That is my type of kid, and those kids tend to be boys."

"I think I respond more empathetically to girls because they are choosing topics that appeal to me, using language that I appreciate, responding to authors I admire, and so it is easier for me to be drawn into their writing," answered Tess Pardini, fifth-grade ESOL (English as a Second or Other Language) teacher in Falls Church, Virginia, and coauthor with Emelie Parker of *"The Words Came Down!" English Language Learners Read, Write, and Talk Across the Curriculum, K–2.*

Other teachers acknowledged that their experiences parenting children of one sex or another also influenced how they responded to boys and girls.

"As a middle school teacher for three years, I know that it has been more challenging for me to relate to the 'boys' boys' in my class, more so than I ever found in lower grades," admitted Cindy Flegenheimer, a sixth/seventh-grade language arts teacher in Washington State. "Overall, I have had to work harder to connect to individual male students than female, although this has become much easier with experience and effort. This is in part because I am female, and may be especially true because, although I have two teens of my own, both are girls."

JoAnn Portalupi points out that how we respond to and evaluate student writing often has as much to do with *us* (our individual tastes and preferences) as what's on the paper. These personal likes and dislikes are quite subjective. You may look for student writing with elaboration and detail; I may be most interested in structure or voice. As writing teachers it is important for us to become aware of our subjective tastes, and try to widen our repertoire.

In a similar way we need to become aware of how gender—ours as well as our students'—impacts us as writing teachers. Yes, in the long run recruiting more men to be K–8 teachers might lead to more writing classrooms that are stimulating to boys. But I do *not* believe that it is necessary to be a male teacher to skillfully teach boy writers.

"I'm female and yes, I do think this affects how I teach and perceive the kids' writing," says Suzanne Whaley, a third-through-fifth-grade reading teacher and coauthor of *Becoming One Community: Reading and Writing with English Language Learners* (Fay and Whaley 2004). "But I try to resist my female slant on things and I purposely try to connect with my boys early on by sharing my own stories and writing about my childhood: getting in trouble with my brother, playing in the woods, being embarrassed at school, etc."

Cyrene Wells works with lower-income middle school students in rural Maine. She found that telling personal stories was a good way to push through the resistance she sometimes feels from the boys.

"I shared a piece about squishing a toad when I was a young child. I poked it so hard that its guts came out, like toothpaste out of a tube. I told them how sick it made me feel, sick and guilty, how it kept me awake at night. After the initial laughter, some of the boys nodded. They knew what it was like." Cyrene recalled other stories she shared. "I read a draft about how much I loved to fly kites when I was a kid and how once I stepped on a big snake as I ran across a field. With appropriate drama, I read how the snake flattened itself across my foot and I admitted that I never wore those shoes again. I never wore the pants I'd been wearing again. And I never flew a kite in that field again, which was the only good place I had for kite flying. The kids and I laughed at my irrational self, but we recognized true feelings. Stories like these got the kids' attention, and I think they helped build trust among us."

What Can I Do in My Classroom?

✖ Consider how your gender might affect how you respond to the substance/style of your boys' writing.

✖ Look at your classroom through the eyes of your boys. What is and isn't working for them in your writing classroom?

✘ Start thinking about how you might revise your teaching (for example, telling high-interest stories like Cyrene Wells did) to show boy writers that you can be on their wavelength, that you are curious and eager to read their writing.

I don't suggest we completely revamp our writing classrooms so they are hand-tailored to fit the needs, styles, and whims of our boys—especially not at the expense of the girls. Rather, let's create the kind of classroom where every boy who enters can say to himself: *This is a place where I can write, a place where I can bring all of myself to my writing.*

The Barrel-Man

Keenan Williams, Grade 5

The Barrel-Man yells, "Let me get some thunder!" Then touchdown number 59! It is the 1991 Denver Broncos against the Green Bay Packers! That's it, the game is over, the Broncos served the Packers!

The Barrel-Man does what he does because his family did it too. So he got some inspiration from that, and because he loves Bronco football games. Plus he's just like most men who love sports—he was just creative with showing it.

After the game the Barrel-Man put down his passport to get his barrel shirt and got ready to leave. He got in the taxi that was waiting for him and they drove to the airport. They reached the airport and he pays the taxi driver 49.50 for the ride. He got in line then, remembers that he left his passport at his house! He races back to the cab and then sped off to his house.

The Barrel-Man wants to go to the game because he hates watching it on TV. Mostly because he can't feel the thundering pound of feet in his barrel. Plus just like my dad he hates commercials because they can be about JC Penny and shoes while it's fourth down and one yard to go. So the Barrel-Man goes in person.

He returns with his passport but his flight had already left for the place the Super Bowl is happening (at Heinz Stadium in Pittsburgh, home of the Steelers). So he asks the taxi driver to drive to Pittsburgh. The taxi driver agrees and they're off again into the waning Sunday night.

The next evening they reach Pittsburgh stadium and hear the loud tune of the Monday night theme song. With a sigh of relief he pays the taxi driver 30,000 dollars and thanks the driver. Then he changes into his barrel shirt and heads for his seat.

Rust crusts the outer regions of the stadium. But while on the inner regions of the bowl the stadium withers with age, and weakness from all the excited fans stomping on it for all these years. Fans are sitting, desperately waiting for the game to start. It feels like the people and the stadium are holding their breaths.

It's the fourth quarter, and the game is almost to a close. The Broncos are down by three points.

The Broncos have the ball at their twenty yard line. Then John Elway throws the ball . . . in John's head he's saying come on, come on, come on! Floyd Little is thinking the same thing and is waiting for the ball to hit his outstretched hands. Droplets of sweat bleed off him like in a shower nozzle. The crowd goes silent and then, a CATCH! In the end zone he catches the ball. The Barrel-Man jumps for joy and steals people's hot dogs and chili fries. He wolfs them down and smashes his beer on the floor. He bangs on his barrel which shakes.

Then the Barrel-Man falls over with the sign of a heart attack. The Barrel-Man was reported dead, for yelling too loud and eating other people's hot dogs and chili fries. To this day we shall remember the Barrel-Man and the stuff he taught us with that barrel. Such as: just do what you want to at programs you love and be that one person who sticks out.

 This unusual profile shows us something we rarely get a chance to see—the life of a sports mascot, in this case for the Denver Broncos. Keenan's story is full of humor and quirky details. It's a great example of characterization. More than anything I love the sheer passion for sports that shines through his piece.

Chapter 4

Rules of (Dis)Engagement

"It's starting to snow!" the teacher said to her class. The fourth graders looked up. "Come over to the windows. We'll open the blinds and take a good look at it."

The kids hurried over, eager to eyeball the year's first snowfall. One boy held back and stayed at his desk.

"Come on, Brent," the teacher urged. "Join us."

But Brent was adamant.

"Don't do it!" he cried to the other kids. "Don't look! She'll make us write!"

Ralph Fletcher, *What a Writer Needs*

Resistance

The *Don't-look-she'll-make-us-write!* anecdote is one of my favorites; it acknowledges the fact that teaching writing is hard work. Not all kids are eager to become authors. Now, in writing this book, I see an obvious fact that had never struck me before—the resister is a boy.

Teachers often find that boys' resistance to writing is hidden but determined, a grassroots insurgency, a sit-down strike. Drop the pencils. Stop the assembly line. We're not gonna crank out any more words. This resistance can take many shapes.

He can never find the draft he's working on.

He keeps sharpening his pencil, then sharpening it again.

He's talking with his friend, who's sitting across the room.

He can whip right through a math sheet, but during writing workshop he always has to go to the bathroom. He's gone for a long time.

"It can be like pulling teeth to get boys to produce anything," says Janet Gilbert, a fourth-grade teacher. "And they can be very creative in not writing: I am thinking about what I am going to write; I have to sketch it first; I can't think of anything to write; he stole my idea; do I have to write about that?"

The resistant, I'm-defeated, I'm-checked-out, I'm-not-gonna-do-this attitude is deadly for the student writer, but it's equally lethal for the classroom as a whole. If you announce: "We're going to start writing time now," and your class groans, well, you're dead in the water. I choose this expression on purpose because it provides an apt metaphor for the energy in writing classroom. When the water is just sitting there a great deal of time, effort, and people power will be required to move it. But once the water is flowing, it's not difficult to dam up one particular part, and redirect the flow.

Flow is a term that was popularized by Mihaly Csikszentmihalyi, a psychologist and author of *Flow: The Psychology of Optimal Experience* (1991). The Flow concept is represented in Figure 4–1.

In this diagram one vector represents the challenge, or required task, being asked of the learner. The other vector represents the student's skills. When the task is too difficult, that is, when the challenge outstrips the learner's skills, that learner will typically become anxious and shut down. (I've experienced this when trying to survive a black diamond trail while skiing with my kids.) If, on the other hand, the task is too easy, the learner will become bored. When the learner's ability roughly matches the task, that student can enter the "flow zone": a perfect storm for learning.

As Csikszentmihalyi describes it, the "flow zone" is a super-rich learning environment where the student becomes totally engaged, so much so that he may lose track of time. The distinction between work and play disappears. In an interview with *Wired* magazine, Csikszentmihalyi described flow as "being completely involved in an activity for its own sake. The ego falls away. Time flies. Every action,

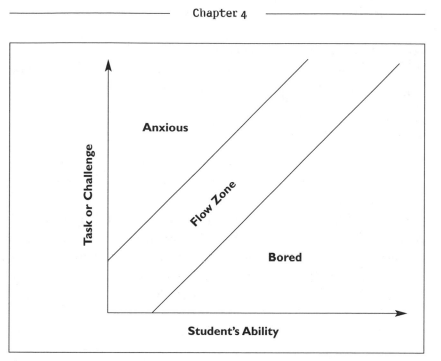

FIGURE 4–1 FLOW DIAGRAM

movement, and thought follows inevitably from the previous one, like playing jazz. Your whole being is involved, and you're using your skills to the utmost" (Geirland 1996).

Smith and Wilhelm make a similar connection between flow and literacy in their book *Reading Don't Fix No Chevys: Literacy in the Lives of Young Men* (2002). Sometimes I think of the "flow zone" as the "comfort zone" we want students to occupy when they write. But right now let's think of it as the *engagement zone*. In a writing classroom this means individual students, and even whole classes, absorbed in writing their stories.

I wondered, when do boys enter this engagement zone when they are *outside* of school? They do seem engaged when they're playing sports or video games, listening to music, riding a skateboard. I can tell when my own sons are in the zone because when I call them for supper, they don't respond; either they don't hear me or choose not to answer.

Next I wondered, when do *boy writers* occupy the flow zone? At first I couldn't think of anything. I do know that millions of teenage boys (and girls) willingly spend hours writing about themselves on popular blog sites such as MySpace. To my knowledge my sons don't do that, although, come to think of it, there is a time when they are so engrossed in the act of writing they completely lose track of time.

Instant Messaging

If a software company developed a program that had millions of kids choosing to write at home, hour upon hour, people would call it a staggering success. Yet that's what is happening. There's a big, sprawling conversation taking place all over the world, a hive of written talk full of news, tips, inside information, gossip, persuasion, future plans, and commentary, and it's called Instant Messaging, or IM. This cyberconversation is so essential that every kid I know wants to be part of it. The desire to IM, in fact, was the number one reason my kids begged us to buy them a computer.

Instant Messaging is hot stuff, but I was slow to catch on. One summer I began to notice my son Robert, who was thirteen, writing messages in little boxes that would appear on the computer screen. When I peered in for a closer look, he'd turn and glare at me, leaving no doubt that he wanted me to leave him alone. Which I did, mostly. I didn't know what he was writing, or who he was writing to. When you visit a website you leave electronic footprints that can be tracked. But IM conversations leave no footprints, don't get saved, and can't easily be retrieved. (The impermanence is, no doubt, a big part of the appeal.) Occasionally one of my sons would leave an IM box open on the desktop of my computer. And, yes, I snooped.

In the following IM dialogue, my youngest son and his friend Laura discuss the film *King Kong*.

```
FireDancerC13: heyy!
Ski4ever1053: Whats up?!
FireDancerC13: not muchhhhhhh:-P
FireDancerC13: how about u
Ski4ever1053: just saw king kong
FireDancerC13: nicee
FireDancerC13: how was it
Ski4ever1053: haha long
Ski4ever1053: but wicked good
FireDancerC13: hahahaahah
```

FireDancerC13: does the gorilla die/
Ski4ever1053: yeah
FireDancerC13: k im not seeing it then
FireDancerC13: thats sad
Ski4ever1053: yeah its wicked sad but he like kills the whole intire
    army before he dies
FireDancerC13: hahaha YEAH BABY thats what i like to see
FireDancerC13: lol
Ski4ever1053: ahha
Ski4ever1053: and he dies because hes like in love with the girl
Ski4ever1053: its confusing
FireDancerC13: omgoshhh
FireDancerC13: thats so sad
FireDancerC13: its like a love story
Ski4ever1053: yeah
FireDancerC13: lol
Ski4ever1053: haha
Ski4ever1053: yeaaaahhhh
Ski4ever1053: haha

I realize that this exchange would offend the sensibilities of most English teachers because it's full of errors and extraneous verbiage. But a closer look into the substance of the dialogue reveals there's more than chitchat going on. Here we see a boy reacting to a popular film, and vulnerable enough to admit his own confusion about what happened. He's using writing as a think-aloud tool.

Some IM conversations seem to possess educational value; others seem chatty and innocuous; still others have a bite that adults may find alarming. A mother I know couldn't resist the urge to read what her eighth-grade son had left on his computer screen.

So you broke up with me—who cares? All u do is make out with guys and then dump them. Congradulations.
    i hate u. u got a little and I really hope you liked it because I garrantee that's all you're getting for the rest of your life!
    i really don't give a f--- if u hate me. [publisher's edit]
    w/e [Whatever.]
    I just feel sorry for the next guy who makes the mistake of going out with u.
    Stop trying to insult me—you're wicked bad at it!

The mother was shocked by the frank, nasty tone of this exchange. She had already made plans to make a two-hour drive to see her mother, and that time allowed her to calm down and reflect on what she had read. It occurred to her that there was probably a certain amount of theater involved in this IM conversation. Her son had written certain things to the girl that he would never say in person. IM provided her son with the armor and the distance for surviving his first breakup with a girl.

I discussed the IM phenomenon with another friend, a woman who is mother to two boys.

"Amazing!" I said. "All these boys who don't like to write in school are choosing to sit at their computer and write like crazy."

She shrugged, unimpressed. "Well, I guess they're motivated to write, if you'd call it that. But it's really just chatting, isn't it? *Hey. Whassup?* That's not what I call writing."

"Why not?" I asked.

"To me, writing is working on a piece that can last, and working on it to improve its quality, to make something good," she said. "IM is nothing like that."

"But it's making these boys into better writers," I replied. "I mean, you can't spend hours working on a skill without getting better at it."

She looked at me skeptically. "Better typists, maybe, but better writers? I don't see it."

Later I considered her point. Of course excellence does matter. We want to help boys develop into strong writers who can clearly communicate their thoughts through precise and nuanced language. But I disagreed with her point that IM writing lacks permanence and, therefore, importance. Would kids agree with her? It's dangerous to breezily dismiss aspects of kids' writing/reading lives. We have done that too often in the past with boys in our classrooms: *Sure, he's reading, but he's stuck on those silly Captain Underpants books. No, he's not writing—he's wasting time drawing pictures for a comic book series he's trying to create.*

When we disregard big chunks of kids' reading/writing lives we risk missing the important stuff. Don't be surprised if ten or twenty years from now many boys look back and cite IM as a key to making writing important to them, a catalyst that helped them see themselves as writers. What is it about the world of IM (the initialism is both a noun and a verb) that makes it such a hothouse for student writing? Some notable characteristics of IM writing include:

✖ *Ferocious fluency.* Kids write fast; I've watched my boys' keyboarding skills increase steadily. Fluency allows their writing to keep abreast of their thinking.

✖ *Quantity.* Twenty years ago research showed that British kids wrote about one hundred words per day, whereas American kids were writing only about one hundred words per week. A writer is someone who writes a lot. I still believe that kids need quantity—frequent, sustained, writing occasions—as well as quality. How can you get better at a skill like skiing, cooking, or yoga if you don't put in the time and do it on a regular basis? When kids are IM-ing they are churning out a high volume of words, plus sustained time on task, without which they cannot become strong writers.

✖ *Strong social component.* Ann Haas Dyson (1993), among others, has convincingly demonstrated the inherent social component to writing. When boys send off an IM they get an almost immediate reaction from the other person. It's like playing catch; one boy tosses a verbal ball to his friend, confident that his friend will throw it back. This social dynamic keeps the energy high, the conversation moving, and the writing flowing.

✖ *Self-directed topic selection.* Choice rules. If someone else brings up a topic that holds little interest for a kid, he can simply sign off, or try to redirect the conversation back to a more interesting issue.

✖ *Experimentation.* Many kids use IM to try on new versions of themselves. It's common for kids to have several screen names, each of them slightly different people, allowing kids to write from various points of view, and try out new writing voices.

Other noteworthy aspects of IM are that it allows kids to:

✖ Get immediate response (not wait a day or two for a writing conference).

✖ Incorporate new vocabulary into their writing.

✖ Express a range of emotions (anger, hurt, concern, boredom).

✖ Discover through actual experience that words have the power to express an idea but also to mislead, hurt, and accidentally make another person angry.

✖ Write at home where they can be comfortable.

✖ Multitask. It's not uncommon for my sons to be IM-ing to a dozen different people all over the country while at the same time working on a homework essay and downloading a song.
✖ Write about high-interest topics.
✖ Have their content/meaning valued over their mechanics.

Private Versus Public Failure

A writer is somebody who is willing to tolerate failure on a massive level. Book by book, page by page, line by line, writers fail and fail. Finally, with enough failure, we find a way to get it right.

The importance of failure resurfaced in "The Trouble with Boys," a *Newsweek* cover article. "Boys measure everything they do or say by a single yardstick: does it make me look weak?" says Michael Thompson. "And if it does, he isn't going to do it." *Newsweek* writer Peg Tyre follows this idea by saying: "That's part of the reason that video games have such a powerful hold on boys; the action is constant, they can calibrate just how hard the challenges will be and, when they lose, the defeat is private" (2006, p. 49).

The idea of private defeat or failure rings true to what I observe in my kids. Joseph is a skateboarder. All through sixth grade he tried to teach himself how to "olley"—a trick in which you jump up, flip the skateboard over, and land on top of it. He had seen other boys do an olley; he desperately wanted to master this skill, but he couldn't do it. He practiced in the garage and, even with the door closed, you could hear from the kitchen as he tried again and again to perfect this trick. I'd know that he had failed yet again because I'd hear the loud yells of frustration and anger. The garage gave him a place where he could fail privately, away from his friends.

Yet month after month Joseph kept trying. At times this persistence seemed almost masochistic. Still, I was impressed. I remembered something I'd heard Katie Ray say about stamina, and how important it is in writing. "I think it's critical: both the stamina of one sitting and the stamina to stay with something over lots of time and keep coming back to it," she said. "Certainly, the stamina of one sitting is critical to testing, but I'm preaching it as being about good writing in general, because I think it's what sets people who get writing done apart from those who talk about getting it done but never do."

Joseph was in that engagement zone. He had all the crucial ingredients: strong interest, the stamina/stubbornness to keep trying,
unlimited time, plus an arena where he could fail safely and privately,
away from the judgmental eyes of his peers. Then one day he came flying into the house, face flushed with success: "I DID IT!"

What implication does this have for writing teachers and the boys
with whom we work? We talk about teach-the-writer-not-just-the-
writing, but I wonder if we really believe that. Or do we expect kids to
"olley" the first time they attempt it? If we truly embraced the importance of failure in learning how to write we might respond differently—less critically—to their early drafts.

What Can I Do in My Classroom?

Clearly the "IM gods" must be doing something right in terms of how
to get boys engaged in writing. You can't help but improve your skills
at anything if you spend an hour or two practicing it every night.
Legions of boys (and girls) are becoming more fluent, more confident,
more alive, and more aware of the power of written words. Of course,
IM is not allowed in most schools. I'm not suggesting we turn our
classrooms into stations where boys do no more than feverishly IM
each other, but perhaps we can borrow aspects of the IM world and
adapt these conditions to our classrooms. Consider these suggestions:

✖ A boy writer must be engaged. This is a nonnegotiable. He must
  feel invested in the writing he is working on. We ignore this
  basic truth at our peril!

✖ Make sure the boys have real and varied audiences for their writing. Sharing and celebrating should not be a rare occurrence but
  a regular event in the classroom.

✖ Create the kind of classroom where boys feel "at home" when
  they write. For instance, let them write on the floor, or in a corner of the room, if that helps them concentrate.

✖ Signal to boy writers that daily, private failure is a necessary
  ingredient for them to become strong writers. We can do this by
  showing examples of professional writers (E. B. White did nine
  drafts of *Charlotte's Web* before it got published), and by sharing
  our own failed drafts. Take a long-term perspective on what they

write. When responding to their writing, our message should not be "You did that wrong," but "I know you learned some things on this piece that will help you on your next piece of writing."

✘ Consider setting up "out of bounds" spaces where kids can do writing that's not for public consumption. For instance, you might allow them to fold over pages in their writer's notebook where the content is personal.

✘ Consider out-of-school writing experiences. Find out what kinds of writing your boys do at home (see "Home Writing Survey," Appendix C). See if you can tap into the energy of that writing and bring it into the classroom.

My sons Robert and Joseph have participated in the Oyster River Players, a local theater group. They have had semimajor roles in plays like *South Pacific*, *As You Like It*, *Annie*, and *The Match Maker*. They have done soliloquies, danced, and sung solos. Watching them perform on the stage I often thought: *This is a side of my boys that teachers never see.* Wouldn't their teachers see them differently if they could see Robert dancing as Bert Healy in *Annie*, or Joseph singing "Consider Yourself" as The Artful Dodger in *Oliver*?

In the same way it's important to remember that we see only a fraction of our boys' lives as readers and writers. IM, emailing, writing on blogs, creating websites, scribbling for fun in notebooks, creating comics with friends—all of these represent an important part of boys' lives as writers. True, some of these arenas are private, but we can inquire and show an interest. Even knowing a little bit about boys' out-of-school writing lives will give us a richer understanding of what engages them as writers.

When I Shot My 0.410

Jimmy Owens, Grade 4

It was quiet. I was on a long dock in Barnwell, SC. 2 by 8's were making x's on every other pole.

Between both docks was an old beaten-up pontoon with no motor.

Old green plastic shingles were on the roof. In one part of the roof was a hole.

One of the floor boards on the dock was loose. The cleat on the floorboard was sort of rusted.

It was just my dad and I.

The tall trees swayed in the faint wind. I took a deep breath.

The air smelled like sweat. Dirt. Fish.

It was warm August weather.

When I picked up the gun, I looked at the barrel.

The barrel looked like it could hold a big shell, but when I opened the barrel the hole for the shell was about a centimeter in diameter.

I grabbed a shell out of my pocket. I slid the shell into the gun real easy. I snapped my back wrist to shut the barrel of the gun.

The gun clicked. My hands were really sweaty.

I was sort of nervous. The gun could go off.

I pulled the gun to my shoulder. I looked down the barrel and aimed for this stump that was probably there before my dad.

I was still sort of nervous. Then my dad said, "Pull the trigger." I pulled the trigger hard. I didn't expect it to be so tight.

The noise was loud enough to make your ears ring.

The sound waves went into the woods and made one long echo. A big wide pattern of lead hit the water and created ripples.

Some pellets hit the stump, but not many. A tiny piece of plastic that kept the lead from crumbling fell into the water.

I let out a sigh, it was like a weight was lifted off of me.

I felt better. It was quiet again.

RF *Jimmy lives in Chapin, South Carolina. His teacher, Gresham Brown, does a fabulous job nurturing boy writers. It's a rite of passage when a boy in the rural South shoots a gun the first time. You can feel that here. What can I say about this poem? Great sense of place at the beginning. I feel like I am standing on the dock beside Jimmy and his father. Jimmy focuses on a brief moment he slowly draws out to reveals its importance. This poem is closely observed and beautifully understated.*

Chapter 5

Vanishing Act:
The Matter of Choice

I wanted to write a scary story but my teacher made me stop writing it. She said it might freak out the class.

Aaron, fourth grade

We are approaching the end of a writing workshop. It's nearly share time, and I have to select which students will get to read their writing out loud to the class. Gazing out, I see kids with pleading faces, frantically waving their hands into the air, begging to be picked.

During writing time I touched base with many kids, so I know the range of what they have written. Matt has written a piece about a wild snowball fight with his cousin Dan. When Matt hid in the shed, Dan threw an ice ball that broke a window, and continued firing snowballs through the broken glass.

Ethan's story is about the morning his cat, Crackers, jumped up on the table and peed into Mom's cup of coffee. It's a story 100 percent guaranteed to crack up the class.

Rachel has written a story about the day she helped her mom defrost the refrigerator six months after her grandmother died. She found a frozen bowl of Grandma's chicken soup, and heated it up. As the family shared the final bowl of soup, they tearfully related stories about Grandma.

Time is scarce; kids go to gym in four minutes. There will be time for only one kid to share. Which student will I choose?

I choose Rachel. And let's be honest: by having this girl stand and read aloud her story I send a blunt message that I value her kind of writing (emotional, poignant, sincere, meaningful) over the kind of writing (plot-driven, violent, low-humor, slapstick) the boys have created.

Topic choice is one of the things that first drew me to the field of process writing. *Kids choose what they want to write about.* This fundamental, democratic tenet of the writing workshop appealed to me on many different levels. It made perfect sense to me as a writer, and I could see how it resonated with young writers. From the first day I worked in schools I watched entire classrooms of kids energized by the freedom to explore what they wanted in their writing.

"We need to encourage our students to bring their obsessions into the classroom," Donald Graves has argued. He said that more than *allowing* topic choice we need to encourage it by showing kids how to "read the world" so they can select workable topics and write well about them.

This feature of the writing workshop (student-selected topics) would seem to be relatively simple and straightforward. But today for boys, it's not simple. Many boys find that the "choice coupon" in the writing workshop contains a great deal of small print listing many types of writing they are *not* allowed to do. Boys get an unfriendly response from their teachers when they try to write about high-interest boy topics such as hunting, favorite movies, comics, outer space adventures, video games, war.

"I created a comic-book character named Wark and loved to write about him in school," Scott, a sixth grader in Epping, New Hampshire, told me. "I got away with it for almost two years, but then my teacher said I couldn't write about him anymore so I had to stop."

Joseph and Jarod, two fourth graders, were big fans of the Redwall books by Brian Jacques. Those books inspired them to create their own series: The Mushroom Wars. They seized on the idea that there would be two armies. The good guys would be edible mushrooms. The bad guys would be toadstools and poisonous fungi. They had a terrific time planning episodes and designing the mushroom soldiers, complete with little helmets and custom weapons. Like Scott, they "got away with it," and managed to work together on this story for two whole days until the teacher found out they were writing a war story and made them stop.

In my survey I asked boys if a teacher had ever "steered you away from something you wanted to write about." Here are some responses from one class in Michigan:

✘ We wrote something inappropriate and she said if we did it again she would call home.

✘ I wanted to write a report about drugs, but my teacher said I'm not allowed.

✘ When my teacher denied my idea on writing a sports story.

✘ Yes, when I make comics with my friend she tells us to stop.

✘ Our teacher said we have to write Rated G but I wanted to write PG.

What is the impact on a boy when his teacher tells him, subtly or explicitly, that what he wants to write about is not welcome in the writing workshop? First he gets angry, resentful. Then he turns off and gives you that "Whatever" look. He glances around the classroom and says to himself: "This writing stuff isn't for me." At the very least he recognizes: "This is not where I can do the real writing." Writing becomes one more example of school's necessary evils, something you have to do even though it doesn't have much value or contain much pleasure.

Some young writers who find their topic choice censored go underground. When my brother Jim and my sister Elaine were in high school in the mid-seventies they started an underground newspaper, *The Bloodthirsty Wolverine*. In it they wrote scathing critiques of the school administration. It's sad that today many boys still have to "go underground," doing the bare minimum in school, waiting until they get home to do the writing they really want to do.

What's going on? Whatever happened to that simple, elegant rule of the writing workshop: *Kids choose what they want to write about*?

The Assault on Choice

Boys in school today find themselves whipsawed by several different forces, each of which limits not just what they can write about but also how they can deal with their topics.

Cultural Fears

"Boys who like to write often say they are working on stories at home, where they can write about what they want," says Carolyn McKinney, a sixth-grade teacher in Pennsylvania. "That's often because what they want to write about is deemed 'inappropriate' in school—especially these days."

"These days" refers to the current political climate of fear in which a No Tolerance weapons policy requires a school district to suspend a kindergarten child who brings a pair of nail clippers into school. In January 2005 two Florida boys, one nine and one ten years old, were arrested and taken from school in handcuffs for making a violent drawing that involved one of their classmates. The 9/11 terrorist attack has made any talking, joking, reading, drawing, or writing about terrorist violence a suspicious act. Tom Newkirk and other writers have pointed out that because of the tragic deaths at Columbine High School, many adults consider boys and their penchant for violent play as a pathology that must be treated, or at least taken very seriously, rather than as a natural (and harmless) developmental stage. This has had a chilling effect on teachers' willingness to allow boys to include firecrackers, gunpowder, knives, or bows and arrows in their stories.

Test Frenzy and Curriculum Mandates

Add to this the wave of assessments (standardized tests) that has swept through education in recent years. In writing instruction this has directly resulted in more writing-to-a-prompt. I worked in one Ohio district where elementary school teachers had students prepare for the forthcoming test in April by writing to a prompt once a week from the very first week of school. A writing curriculum so heavily slanted toward test preparation will not encourage kids to develop a love for writing, find their voices, and deeply engage in the craft.

Some educators insist that test or prompt writing is necessary, but we should also consider what impact all this test preparation has on the attitudes of boy writers. Not only are we force-feeding them a kind of writing that is teacher-directed and formulaic, but, more important, there's no payoff—no purpose, no tangible reader, no fun—for the writer who struggles to create such a text. The only payoff I can imagine is to get the test writing done.

But high-stakes testing alone isn't responsible for the disappearance of choice in writing classrooms. State by state, the curriculum has become narrower and more circumscribed. The profusion of new curricular mandates encourages teachers to try to "kill two birds" with one stone—cover the content by assigning kids to write about it. This leaves less and less time for student-generated topics. Take the writer's notebook. The notebook should be a bastion of student choice, but more and more teachers use it as a place where kids practice teacher-directed skills and strategies, not at all how I envision the writer's notebook.

The problem has deep roots. How can teachers give students the opportunity for real choice and experimentation when teachers themselves are forced to teach a curriculum defined in such rigid ways?

Today in many classrooms teachers lead students through genre studies or "units of study" in which kids are directed to write in a particular form. Certainly these content-rich units of study can help students gain a deeper understanding of various genres. But there's also a cost—these units of study whittle away at the student's choice. When poorly implemented they can lead to a scenario in which students are working in a poetry unit of study and the teacher announces: "Today we're going to be writing poems about spring." In this case both genre *and* topic are determined by the teacher. To put it mildly, this is not my idea of writing workshop.

Boys crave choice when they write. I surveyed nearly five hundred boys, trying to unearth their attitudes and experiences about writing, both in and out of school. At the end of the survey I asked them to complete this sentence: "When we write in school I wish we were allowed to . . ." The overwhelming response to this question was a plea for more choice.

> Create our own topic.
> Choose.
> Write whatever we want.

Here's a radical idea: let's bring choice back to the writing classroom. Just let them write. I don't know a better first step to create an environment that will engage our boy writers.

"Many times my strongest writers are boys," says Bruce Morgan, "*if* I can get them to write what they really *want* to write and if they will take the time to work hard enough to create something great."

"Many boys really believe writing is not for them and this has been reinforced to them for years by their teachers, whether the teachers realize it or not," observes Dennise O'Grady, a teacher in New Jersey. "Once boys are given some space to simply write, it becomes much easier to see their natural bent and then go in and teach them some craft that really is connected to what they are already doing. And then, boys are so open and willing to take risks with what you give them. They need to see the relevance in what they are already doing."

What Can I Do in My Classroom?

✗ Consider specific steps to give students more choice in what they write. For example, if you ask kids to write in genre studies or units of study, which direct student choice, you can also schedule "Open Cycles" or "Free Choice Zones" from time to time where kids have complete choice in bringing their interests and obsessions into the writing classroom.

✗ Find out what your boys really care about, and encourage them to write about those topics (even if they are not subjects that fascinate you). This doesn't have to be limited to blood 'n' guts but might also include race car driving, repairing a dirt bike, building a skateboarding ramp, fishing, profiles of rock musicians, professional wrestlers, and so forth.

✗ Widen the circle one notch, and be more generous about what pieces get read aloud during share time.

✗ Remember that choice involves not just the *what* but the *how*. Giving students more choice in the *how* might include allowing them to be conversational, use slang or words from a native language, employ humor, include illustrations, or write with an authentic, childlike voice ("Me and my brother went swimming . . .") even if that means the writing is ungrammatical.

In any classroom there will be a natural tension between the adult culture/values/norms of the teacher and the students. The next two chapters examine two major flashpoints that arise whenever boys write, or try to write, in school.

Rocks

Paulus Abuakel, Grade 5

p. 1

"Hey Bob," said Hank, looking at the beautiful rock. "Check this out."

Bob examined it. "Where'd you find it?"

"Over there in that cave," said Hank, pointing at the cave. So they both went in the cave. After awhile, they saw the same rock. Hank said, "We going to be richer than Bill Gates!"

Can you guess what rock Hank found?

Hint! It's the hardest rock.

If you guessed diamond, then you are correct! Diamonds really are the hardest rock. If you find a diamond, you could report it to the news, tell your parents, sell it, keep it, or keep it a secret.

p. 2

Who likes to watch Smallville? Well, if you do, you probably know that Kryptonite is Clark Kent's weakness. Kryptonite isn't a real rock but it's a rock. Now there is such an element called Krypton (KR). Krypton is where Clark Kent was born. Then the meteors came and he got his human parents.

Now meteors are rocks too but bigger maybe a lot bigger or smaller but they fall fast. If it hits earth a crater will form.

p. 3

Did you know that our rocky earth weights 6 sextillion, 588 quintillion tons? (6,588,000,000,000,000,000,000).

If I got that money for free I don't know what I'd do with it.

This is an excerpt of a much longer report on rocks. Paulus makes his topic come alive with playful drawings, a narrative lead, references to pop culture, and occasional wisecracks to the reader. This topic could be dry and boring, but the skillful writing makes it a pleasure to read.

Rocks

Writen by Paulus Abuakel

Ilistrated by Paulus Abuakel

Kryptonite

I am weakining

meator

crator

Who likes to watch Smallville? Well, if you do, you probably know that Kryptonite is Clark kent's weakness. Kryptonite isn't a real rock but it's a rock. Now there is such an element called Krypton (KR) Krypton is were Clark Kent was born then the meators came and he got his human parents.

Now meators are rocks to but bigger mabye alot bigger or smaller but they fall fast. If it hits earth a crator will form.

Chapter 6

Violent Writing

If writing is truly an expression of ideas and feelings, and boys are allowed to express themselves, we will see more aggressive and physical kinds of expression.

Janet Gilbert, fourth-grade teacher

Artie Voigt, my friend and colleague, once gave me this advice about raising boys: "Get them involved in the most dangerous sport you can find: football, boxing, skiing, something like that. It's got to be dangerous, and it's got to be supervised."

For boys in school, writing could fit the bill—a dangerous, supervised sport. Why couldn't the writing workshop be an arena where we could guide boys as they use writing to grapple with dangerous issues? Unfortunately, that doesn't happen in most classrooms because many teachers are uncomfortable when boys weave violence into their stories, which they often do.

"Teachers tend to thwart the boys from writing war stories," notes Marianne Norman, a writing consultant in Indiana. "I have noticed that boys tend to write stories based on some of their favorite video games. Those get a bit violent. But that's where they live!"

I vividly remember my son Robert, who was four years old at the time, sitting at the kitchen table wearing a worn He-Man T-shirt he had inherited from an older brother.

"I love violence," Robert said. He made this announcement in a merry voice, his hazel eyes twinkling, fully aware that such a remark would leave his parents deeply perturbed, which it did. In our family we don't own any guns, support stronger gun control, and make a serious effort to regulate how much unfiltered violence our kids are exposed to in video games, movies, and TV shows.

Despite our antigun, antiviolence stance (or maybe *because* of it) Robert was strongly attracted to weapons. Nothing we did seemed to douse his passion. He wanted to talk about weapons; he asked for toy swords and toy guns for Christmas; he never failed to incorporate them into his drawings and stories. One of his favorite books was *The Fox Went Out on a Chilly Night* by Peter Spier. Whenever I read it to him he'd stop sucking his fingers just long enough to point out the ancient cannon in the village square.

JoAnn was more troubled than I was by Robert's interest in weapons. She forbade toy guns in the house, but that didn't stop Robert. One day he took his lunch sandwich, pulled off some of the bread, and created his own "gun sandwich," which he gleefully pointed at his older brothers.

When you ask people about boys and violence, opinions are split about whether it's a matter of nature (boys born with a predisposition toward violence) or nurture (boys shaped by society's image of males). I would never discount the impact of images put forth by the media and male roles/expectations that boys soak up in their families. Still, I happen to lean toward nature, and believe that most boys have a natural interest in such topics.

I know I did. There's a chapter in *Marshfield Dreams: When I Was a Kid* (Fletcher 2005) titled "War" that describes the game I most loved to play. In the game as we played it, the most important part of War was knowing how to die. Today, vicious, ultrarealistic battle scenes in movies like *Braveheart, Black Hawk Down,* or *Saving Private Ryan* make me cringe. But I sure loved playing war as a kid.

Like me, most boys pass through their guns-and-war stage and grow out of it. I would make the same argument for violent writing.

The issue of violent writing is, of course, inextricably tangled with the issue of choice. In my written survey I asked teachers: "What do your boys like to write about?" Here are some replies I received, verbatim:

aliens, monsters, horror stories
hero stories (usually fantasy or war-related)
war, violence, drugs
"thug"/fighting/gun stories
war and military situations that involve guns/ammo or equip-
    ment such as jets, planes, tanks, trucks
accidents and injuries
mistakenly hurting someone else
something awful that has happened in their life
teams, sports, and the feeling of confidence they get from sports
dislike for school and/or certain mean teachers they feel have
    misunderstood them
driving cars or snowmobiles, dirt bikes, four-wheelers
places they know, trips, pets, collections
video games, movies, cartoon-related stories (DragonBallZ)
fiction stories—Captain Underpants–like and superheroes
popular movie figures, typically action figures
activity with their fathers: fishing, hunting, sports events
actual adventures with friends in which parents were not around
    (meeting a moose on the way to school, snowball fights)
adventure parks (waterslides, roller coasters, thrill rides)
toys and electronic games (Power Rangers, Batman, etc.)
a physical challenge
tough characters juxtaposed with softer characters
fantasy worlds (often stems out of popular literature)
grandiose ideas that seem big enough for a two- to three-hour
    feature film or a seven-hundred-page novel
rescue vehicles (helicopters and fire engines)
robots, fighting and destroying evil characters, etc.
computer/video games

Anyone who has worked with boys will recognize these topics. The writing about such subjects tends to be heavy on action and conflict. In general it will not be very introspective, ruminative, or deep in character analysis. Looking at this list, it occurs to me how often aggression and violence (blood, fighting, attacking, killing) are a part of these topics. Stripped of violence and physical conflict, they would be lifeless indeed.

I asked one fifth-grade teacher how she deals with violence in boys' writing. "I don't allow blood and guts," she confided, "so I don't have that problem." Maybe not, but I would argue that if you outlaw all "boy topics" you end up with a very watered-down menu, at least from a boy's point of view (see Chapter 15), which creates a more serious problem—a room full of turned-off boys.

My nephew Santiago, a second grader, lives near Washington, D.C. My uncle John Collins lives nearby in Maryland. Growing up we always called him "Johnny the Soldier." Uncle John lied his way into World War II as a seventeen-year-old, fought in the Battle of the Bulge, earned two Purple Hearts. Later he fought in the Korean War. In the summer my sister takes Santi to Uncle John's house, and they go fishing. At home Santi often writes war stories that include elaborate drawings of tanks, planes, and bombs. In school he's not allowed to write about war. I asked Santi what he most wished about writing in school.

"When we write in school I wish we were allowed to write about World War II," he says, "because my great-uncle was in that war."

Why should boys be prohibited from writing about war? Many writers—Wilfred Owen, Stephen Crane, Ernest Hemingway—have created enduring works of literature that deal with war. Directors have done the same thing in film. Obviously boys writing at this level will not reach the quality or lofty themes found in those works; nevertheless, the subject certainly provides rich material for writers of any age.

There's another reason we should make more room for this kind of writing. In *Misreading Masculinity* (2002) Tom Newkirk makes an interesting argument for the social role violence can play in boys' writing. He points out that when girls write it's allowable to directly express affections: "Judy is my best friend. The many secrets we keep between us are treasured in my heart. . . ."

"Boys are different," writes Leonard Sax in *Why Gender Matters*. "Most boys don't really want to hear each other's innermost secrets. With boys the focus is on the activity, not the conversation" (2005, p. 83).

William Pollack, author of *Real Boys: Rescuing Our Sons from the Myths of Boyhood* (1998), says that an expression of affection isn't allowable in boys' writing. Pollack argues that the "boy code" prevents it because it makes boys look weak or vulnerable. Instead, boys are apt to write action stories filled with danger and violence, in which the characters go through an exciting experience together and triumph over difficult obstacles. For boys, violent writing provides an important way of bonding and expressing friendship. Look at this story written by Thomas Surtevant, a fifth grader from Waterville, Maine.

Beautiful Fights

It was a Friday night. Thomas Sturtevant and his friend Chad are going to a Portland Pirate game. They love fights! Well, let's hurry up and get to the good part.

"It is really chilly for a Friday night in May, isn't it?"

"Ya," said Chad.

When they got in the rink they heard CRACK! The lights have gone out! An hour later the game is back on! In the first few seconds Shawn passed to Mo. Shot! Goal!

Then the best part happened! A fight! Jordan and a goalie! Then both teams were on the ice! Bang! Chang threw the first punch! Shawn and Chad were in a fight! This was no ordinary fight. Both teams were on the ice. And to make it even better, now the crowd is part of the fight! Helmets flying, skates slashing faces, gloves flying like pistols. I can't feel my legs. Then I see a big pile of blood but then the fight ended when a cop fired his gun, BANG.

The bad part of the bloodthirsty game is that Howard was suspended and the rest of the team, too. The next day Thomas and Chad were in the hospital because they had broken legs, arms, and collar bones.

Thomas said: "It is worth breaking every bone in your body to be in a fight."

"I wonder who won," Chad said.

Thomas said, "Portland, I think. Come on, share the remote!"

"Fine! Click!"

Here we see two boys unapologetically reveling in their passion: hockey fights. The title says it all. "Beautiful Fights" isn't a realistic narrative but a fantasy where instead of merely watching a hockey brawl the boys actually get to participate in one. What could be better than that? At the end we see the two warriors in the hospital, battered but happy, wrestling over the TV remote. It could never be stated directly but it's apparent that this experience has brought them closer together.

In summary, I'd argue three reasons for allowing boys more latitude in incorporating violence into their writing in school:

✗ A wider zone of engagement—the boys will be more invested in their writing and in the workshop as a whole when they see that they can bring their passions into it.

✗ Through written language they can safely grapple with power and danger, issues that make up a big part of a boy's internal world.

✗ Social capital—violent writing is classroom currency that can be "spent" and used to bond with friends.

When it comes to violence I'm suggesting we give boys more latitude, but I don't believe that carte blanche choice should be given in the writing classroom. Choice is *negotiated* between students and teacher, and this negotiation should take into account that there's a built-in culture (and gender) clash between the student's world and the world of the teacher. There must be commonsense limitations on how much violence we permit in student writing. Boys who play the Grand Theft Auto video game, or hum along to ultraviolent rap lyrics, may go too far in their writing. Isoke Nia, who is sympathetic to the idea of giving boys more latitude with topic choice, points out that every teacher has to draw the line between what is acceptable and what is truly offensive.

"Often boys write about useless violence (many times against women)," Isoke says. "This I stop. I call these stories 'kick-um-in-the-head stories,' and I explain to the students that there is enough violence in the world and we are going to be the kind of people who push away from the violence even in our writing."

Dangerous Words

There's another kind of boy writing that makes us uncomfortable even if it is not explicitly violent. The following piece was written by a seventh-grade boy:

School. My school is one a huge hill. But how does it stand up? There's a big chamber under the hill. The teacher's teach for 6 hours and 30 minutes. They suck the fun out of you and make a thick layer of hot rising gas. It makes your school stand up. Most the teachers do it well, and they're Evil. They teach stuff that you forget 2 minutes later. When you have a test, you're in trouble. The teachers make you take so many notes, you can't find the one your looking for. Then you make so many spelling erors it's not even funny. Even day is missery, doing pages and pages of work. I need a break every two years, you know? Even in the Cafeteria, there's live pea monster in your lunch. School is torcher, especially literacy. They give you the most boring information you could amagen. They put you in a cage til your 36. In college you get 3 hours of homework. Even in 4th grade you get 3 hours of homework a lot. Huh? Yeah, I need a break, a two year long Break from My Boring School.

Writing like this certainly does not make us sigh and go misty-eyed. It's edgy, snide, and confrontational. It makes us uncomfortable and suggests an unpleasant, even disturbing point of view we'd rather not face. This boy is "challenging the gods." It's not the kind of pretty piece most teachers would be eager to read aloud in the writing workshop, but it's certainly strong and it is full of voice.

Sometimes writing can be dangerous for yet another reason. I worked in a third-grade class where a boy named Max wrote a story that had this first line: "Thank God my Dad finally joined AA!" What followed was a brutally honest narrative recounting the pain of his father's drinking, and how it had affected the family.

"I can see that this is really important to you," I told Max.

"Yeah," he agreed, "things are a lot better in the house now that Dad joined AA."

"You know, the second *A* in AA is *Anonymous*," I pointed out. "That means when nobody knows the name of the person. Your dad has a right to his privacy with something like this."

I helped Max find a place in the corner, away from the other kids, where he could complete his story. When he finished it, I mentioned again the issue of privacy. I suggested that we put his story away and not share it out loud with the class, and Max agreed.

On occasion a teacher may have to draw the line when a student uses offensive language, or writes about something revealing, sexually explicit, or gruesomely violent. When a student does cross the line in his writing, we need to be thoughtful about how we respond.

"If a boy writes something questionable I usually just talk to him about it," Suzanne Whaley says. "'So, what were you thinking about when you wrote this? Where did you get the idea?' Usually it comes out that they're playing around with characters, plot, voice, and language.

Sometimes I've misread a word and my interpretation of the piece is way off because of a misspelled word."

Suzanne's final point is an interesting one—often our initial reading causes us to misinterpret or misread the substance of the writing. Before we react in a hostile fashion, it's important to carefully reread and make sure we have read what we thought we read.

"There have been a handful of incidents where the kids pushed the envelope to see my tolerance level," says Max Brand, a fifth-grade teacher in Dublin, Ohio, and author of *Word Savvy*. "A short conference that is not threatening, asking about why they wrote what they wrote, and if they felt it was appropriate, usually will stop the momentum. Hostility is definitely not helpful. Helping the kids save face is paramount."

What Can I Do in My Classroom?

If we truly want to get boys writing, we must give them a wider engagement zone in the workshop. My suggestions:

✖ Don't automatically outlaw stories with weapons.

✖ Think carefully about what language is deemed allowable in their writing. Most boys know how to code-switch between what they do and say on the street and what fits into the school culture. But you might want to put forth some reasonable guidelines. One teacher I know made a distinction between the classroom, the playground, and the street.

"When you write you can certainly use the kind of language you'd use in the classroom," she said. "And I don't mind if you use the language you'd use on the playground. But some of the stuff we hear on the street—I think we can live without that." The boys seemed comfortable with that and didn't cross the line.

✖ Think about language *we* use to talk about this issue. Revisit all the cut-and-dried rules about what students are allowed to include in their writing. Bring kids into the dialogue. The best classroom rules evolve from a discussion in which every student, plus the teacher, has a voice.

✖ Try not to judge students by what they write. Accept it, and help them make the writing better.

✘ Look for well-written texts (novels by Gary Paulsen, stories by
   Edgar Allan Poe) that model skillful use of violence in a narrative.

✘ Look for the humor underneath the violence. As we'll see in the
   next chapter, much of the violent writing we see from boys may
   actually be humor in disguise.

When boys incorporate violence in their writing some teachers
consider it a form of acting out or misbehaving. (Boys who get caught
often are forced to write for punishment.) But I believe that violent
writing is actually important to their development. Bruno Bettelheim
argued that children need to hear the "real" fairy tales, even though
such stories can be frightening and gruesome. Those tales allow kids
to get in touch with the terror of being a child. In a similar way, violent writing allows boys to understand and express the basic male narrative: they are young men growing toward the age when many men
around the world must go to war. Even if they don't become soldiers
they will become heads of households. They will walk in their fathers'
shoes. They must take their places in a dangerous world.

Baseball

Ryan Braley, Grade 2

I'm playing baseball this season. I love baseball, I play every year. Baseball is a good and healthy sport. I am on the Rockiest. Travis, Josh, and that's all I remember that are on my team. I'm totally ready for baseball. On the Red Sox there are Matt H. and Seth and that's all I remember. Travis's dad is the coach. His name is Mark. Mark is cool. He's a nice guy. But I don't get to see him much. He's a very good coach. I'm thinking this year is going to be a good year. I'm ready to hit a thousand homeruns. I'm realy good at slugging, and I can turn a single into a double in a blink of an eye. I'm always prepared for anything. Last year in minor my cousin pitched the ball and hit my ankle it hurt a lot. but I was alright. I think baseballs cool. I think other people do to. I'm never removed from baseball. Me and baseball are like family. It runs in my blood. My favorite player is Johnny Damon. He used to be on the Redsox now he is on the Yankees. I hate Yankees In almost every way. I also have a baseball video game. I went to a Redsox game last year. I'm going to another one this year. Actually two. I love the Redsox they are cool. What kind person doesn't like to play baseball and exercicise. It's very fun. It stinks in winter I don't get to play. I play kickball to the rules are the same. Acept that you have roll instead of pitch. and kick instead of bat. I hope Baseball is a sport to the world forever. The End.

What a sweet piece! Ryan has written a kind of love letter to baseball. It's a rambling stream-of-consciousness sort of piece, and we might be tempted to help him organize it with paragraphs until we realize that he's only in second grade. I love the voice here. As I read it I find sentences that are profound: "I'm never removed from baseball."

Chapter 7

Humor

Boys are more willing to break the rules to get a laugh, to get bawdy. I think boys are a bit like Shakespeare tragedies, capable of profundity but also more able to easily reach the rabble with low humor and crudity. Boys need more slack to discover meaningful topics and the freedom to explore silly ones.

Barry Lane

One morning my son Robert, who was in third grade, glared at me from the kitchen table.

"Hey, Dad, get me some cereal!" he ordered.

"Robert!" I frowned at him. "Is that any way to talk to your father?"

"I forgot the magic words," he said with a mischievous smile. "OR I'LL SUE YA!"

When visiting schools I often retell the Or-I'll-sue-ya anecdote. Robert's irreverent remark never fails to bring down the house. The boys, especially, howl with laughter.

"Don't you think that was a little . . . rude?" I ask them.

"Yeah," one boy admitted. "But it's still wicked funny!"

Recently I made an author visit to Dover Middle School in Dover, New Hampshire, not far from where I live. One class filed into the

61

auditorium early. The teacher stepped out, leaving me and the students to wait for the other classes to arrive. For a long awkward moment those students and I stared at each other.

"You guys are in eighth grade, huh?" I asked.

The students nodded.

"How are you doing?" I asked, trying to be friendly.

At first nobody answered. Then one boy spoke up.

"Peachy," he said dryly. The other kids laughed, approving of a boy who took a chance to act cheeky to an adult, especially a guest who was supposed to be some kind of VIP.

A few years ago I would have considered Robert's comment and this boy's remark insolent, sarcastic, rude. Writers like William Pollack, Leonard Sax, Michael Thompson, and Tom Newkirk have helped me see them in a broader context. They refer to the "boy code," which, in an institution such as school, compels boys to resist any rule enforcer who wields the power. This boy's sassy rejoinder was his way of telling me: "Don't think that I chose to come to this assembly, because I didn't. Don't assume that I'm going to make nice with you, because I'm not."

Boys revel in subversive humor, a form of humor that requires a certain amount of risk taking. Although such humor can seem impolite, it represents a major way boys can demonstrate their independence and resist authority.

"Humor levels the playing field," Barry Lane suggests. "And most schools are more hierarchical than they would like to admit."

Years ago I got into a conversation about burial arrangements with my son Adam, who was about seventeen at the time.

"I don't want to be embalmed," I said emphatically. "I want my body to be cremated after I die, okay?"

"Okay." He grinned and winked at me. "I'll light the match myself."

Writing teachers seem reasonably tolerant with oral humor because spoken words dissolve quickly into the air. The moment passes; we all move on. Humor in writing is a different matter because written words are permanent, an indelible relic that others (teachers, principals, parents) can seize upon and criticize. Teachers often feel judged by "how far kids go" when they write. Maybe that explains why many teachers react in hostile ways to humor in boys' writing.

I have a friend who wanted to write a book about teaching kids how to write humor. He sent it to a well-known publisher and his proposal got sent out to a reviewer. Four weeks later he received the reviewer's comments, which were not encouraging.

"Frankly, humor is not something I like to encourage in the classroom," the reviewer said, "especially among boys who see crude humor as an opportunity to become the center of attention."

In a recent book for kids about my composing process I explained that in school I always thought writers had to dream up imaginary things to write about. In fact, actual events from your life often provide terrific material for stories and poems. As an example I included in my original manuscript the following true story:

When I lived in Marshfield, Massachusetts, we had roosters. They were nice enough pets, but they crapped all over the yard. Next door to us lived a five-year-old named Sammy, a boy who was extremely gullible. One day Tom, my most devious younger brother, put some chicken crap on the end of a stick and offered it to Sammy.

"You should try this," Tom suggested. "It's tasty!"

To my utter disbelief and before I could stop him, Sammy opened his mouth and let Tom insert the poopy stick. Sammy's eyes flew wide open. He spit it out, turned, and raced into the house, bawling at the top of his lungs. Tom ran in the opposite direction toward our house.

This is perhaps the most famous story we have in our family, one that has been retold many times. (My brother Tom got an old-fashioned whipping for pulling this stunt.) When my editor returned the manuscript she put a big red flag next to this section. Later she phoned to discuss it.

"You've got to take that part out," she declared.

"Why?" I asked.

"Look, I taught in public schools," she said. "Believe me; as soon as the teacher reads that part out loud the kids will be in an uproar."

"You think so?" I asked.

"Not the kids," she corrected herself. "The boys! The boys will be absolutely gone, screaming with laughter, rolling on the floor. It'll take at least twenty minutes for the poor teacher to regain control of the class!"

At this point in the conversation I found myself in the position of having to fight for the chicken shit, which seemed pretty absurd, so I reluctantly agreed to remove this anecdote from the book. That evening I told my wife what had happened. JoAnn was dismayed.

"But you're censoring a high-interest part of the book before it has even been published!" she exclaimed.

As much as I hated to admit it, I could see she was right. The next day I happened to bump into Tom Newkirk at my local post office. I told him the story, too.

"The boys would be 'rolling on the floor,'" Tom repeated, sadly shaking his head. "God forbid we have a book in the classroom that's so funny and engaging it would get a bunch of boys rolling on the floor!"

This story involved female editors. In fact, all the editors I have had in the past fifteen years have been women. I have learned a great deal from these editors; I value them tremendously. Still, this experience left me with at least two nagging questions: How much of a part, if any, did our different genders play in the clash between our conflicting aesthetics? How can boys envision themselves as writers if they don't find in books they read examples of the strong, salty writing they want to create themselves?

Whatever the answers, I was left with one disturbing thought: surely the revision I made resulted in a published book that is a little less interesting, a little less engaging to boy readers.

This widely held sentiment about boys and humor is unfortunate. It's not merely that boys respond to humor and find it entertaining. Humor is a milieu in which boys thrive.

"I like to write funny," said Cole, a fifth grader who explained that humor is his favorite genre to write.

Griffin, a fourth-grade boy, told me: "I can't believe how much I've learned from watching *South Park*!" This comment surprised me—I admit that I have never thought shows like *South Park* and *The Simpsons* have much educational value. But Griffin insisted that he had learned a great deal about history, law, war, politics, government, and the environment from watching that show.

Taylor, our oldest, would agree. He still claims he picked up most of what he learned about history by reading *Dave Barry Slept Here: A Sort of History of the U.S.* (Barry 1997).

Boys want to "write funny" because they love to "read funny." Some of the crass humor in their writing (burping, farting, dirty diapers) tries our patience, but many boys are simply making "text-to-text" connections between their writing and the kind of humor they read in books like the Captain Underpants series by Dav Pilkey (which boys universally adore) or *Zombie Butts from Uranus!* by Andy Griffiths—books that revel in bathroom humor. Also, boy writers are strongly influenced by popular mainstream films such as *Anger Management, School of Rock,* or *Meet the Parents,* which are loaded with lowbrow comedy.

When it comes to humor in writing, there will always be an inherent clash between adult culture and child culture. Recently I sat with some fourth-grade teachers while they read a pile of stories written by boys.

"These two are pretty silly," one teacher said dismissively. "But *this* one is really funny."

I wondered: Who gets to decide what writing is funny? And why must "silly" be relegated to the bottom rung of the comedy ladder? If I have learned anything about writing for kids I have learned that kid humor is distinctly different from adult humor. For instance, in *Flying Solo* (1998) I included one character who keeps saying "Fact" or "Opinion" to whatever comments the other students made. Adults are bemused by this idea—kids find it hysterical. I got the idea from our oldest, Taylor, who did the very same thing when he was in fifth grade on a family car trip. This was amusing at first, but after three hours my patience wore thin.

"Taylor, you're driving me crazy," I finally told him.

"Opinion?" he asked, giggling.

"Fact!" I told him. "Stop it!"

In *Misreading Masculinity* Tom Newkirk makes a serious case for slapstick and crude humor, pointing out that such forms of humor appear in classic literature from Beowulf to Shakespearean theater. "Low comedy" resonates with boys; no wonder they want to experiment with it in their writing. On occasion I have incorporated this brand of humor into my own novels, including this passage in *Flying Solo:*

> *"Yes, I shall read my masterpiece!" Christopher declared proudly.*
> *"You will now hear the Legend of Sir Francis Brave Fart!"*
>
> > *"Braveheart?" Robert asked.*
>
> > *"No, Brave* Fart*!" Christopher said, and started reading.*
>
> > On the night before the great battle Sir Francis Brave Fart came to dinner with a legion of other fearless knights. As he

sat down on a chair he suddenly farted and the chair exploded in a cloud of foul smoke.

> *The boys cracked up.*
> *"You moron," Jasmine said.*
> *"Opinion!" Christopher giggled. He read:*

The other knights were stunned and excited. They had finally found a secret new weapon that might work in their bloody war against the all-powerful Dark Knight! *(p. 65)*

After students finish reading *Flying Solo*, they often mention this passage to me.

"Why did you put in the part about Sir Francis Brave Fart?" one boy asked. I guessed his thoughts: he could never write such a thing in his school writing. So how did *I* manage to get away with it?

Humor and Violence

Often the humor in a boy's story gets overshadowed or obscured by violence in the plot. Consider this a piece written by Sean, a fifth-grade writer:

> *There was this guy living in a place like Kansas or Oklahoma. He was living in a trailer which was a big mistake—everybody knows that trailers are tornado magnets. So anyway this tornado comes down and starts sucking the guy out of his trailer. He's screaming like murder, trying to hold on, but he finally lets go. He goes flying through the air but a board hits him and cuts the guy's head in two pieces. I guess you could say he had a splitting headache—hah! The guy fell into a ditch but he didn't know that it was a live training ground for the U.S. Army. "Incoming!" someone screamed to the unfortunate dude, but it was much much too late.*

In the old days a story like this containing war and split-open heads would definitely make me uncomfortable. If Sean had written it during a writing workshop, and had wanted to share it, I probably would have prevented him from doing so. Directly or indirectly I'd send the message: this kind of writing is not appropriate in school.

But a closer look at this piece reveals a surprising degree of skill. The narrator's irreverent tone pulls us in. At the beginning we get a dose of fresh, sly humor (trailers as "tornado magnets") that grabs us. Yes, the piece does contain a lot of violence. But like a Quentin Tarantino movie, the violence is so relentless it almost feels like a comic book. At some point we realize that we are not meant to take this violence seriously.

Newkirk points out that a James Bond film often contains violence that is undercut and softened by humor. You can see an example of that in this writing sample when the board cuts the man's head in two and gives him a "splitting headache." Sean has written an edgy piece full of irreverent humor that makes me want to keep reading. Isn't that a touchstone of effective writing?

In addition to violent humor (or humorous violence), boys love to write satire and spoofs, writing that deliberately insults, challenges, raises eyebrows, shakes up our staid perspectives. The power of this genre comes from its irreverence, its mockery of society as we know it. Satirical writers have a long and distinguished history, and include practitioners such as Thomas Paine, Jonathan Swift, and P. J. O'Rourke.

"Boys seem to enjoy parody, farce, and off-color humor more than girls," says Andrea Morgan, a fifth-grade teacher in Denver. "If you give them a little leeway with this, you get more writing!"

But we cannot nurture what we can't understand. Many teachers are not so much hostile to as honestly perplexed by boy humor in boy writing.

"A big issue for me is that I don't always share their sense of humor so I can't really follow some of their writing," admits Franki Sibberson, fourth-grade teacher and coauthor of *Beyond Leveled Books: Supporting Transitional Readers in Grades 2–5*. "I read it and think no one will understand it, then they share with the class and it gets huge laughter and response. I can't figure out if they are responding to one funny line or if there is some plot line that I am not picking up because to me, so much is missing."

"The biggest problem is that I don't get it," agrees Carolyn McKinney, a sixth-grade teacher. "Many boys are really into that obvious and simplistic humor, and I often find myself saying, 'That's funny?' When I ask why, they often reply: 'I don't know, it's just funny.' This creates a conflict of interest between boys and teachers of writing, because teachers often feel the boys are not 'applying themselves,' or taking their work seriously when they write in this fashion."

What Can I Do in My Classroom?

Being friendlier to boys' humor is an important way we can widen the circle and invite boys to be full citizens in our writing classrooms. This starts with recognizing what they are trying to do in this regard.

✖ If boys want to "write funny" encourage them to examine texts such as *The Dumb Bunnies* by Dav Pilkey, or any of the Jon Scieskza picture books, for what makes these books humorous.

✖ Before you outlaw a particular kind of boys' humor, make sure you understand it. Recognize that your appraisal of boys' humor often reveals as much about you as it does about the writing.

✖ Take your boys' humor seriously. Look for the intelligence behind the apparent silliness.

✖ Try using a new mental language for your thinking on this subject. Instead of "humor," think "voice." Instead of "silly," think "satire."

✖ Be as generous as possible with their humor. Make a distinction between what's destructive and what is merely irreverent. When students step over the line (and they will), take it on a case-by-case basis.

✖ Give yourself permission to enjoy their humor. Boys really can be funny. Laugh!

Boys who include humor in their writing are not necessarily acting out, fooling around, or trying to get attention. Rather, humor gives them a crucial way to express their authentic voices. This is certainly true for me. I make presentations to teachers and if I were not allowed to interject any humor into my talks they would be impoverished indeed. Using humor is more a way to keep things from getting dull; it is a part of who I am, a crucial slice of my heart. It gives me a way of expressing the absurd human dilemma of being a finite mortal being in an infinite universe.

Origami

Chris Minafo, Grade 5

Origami. as I read I think what comes next? aw . . . fold the top corner over the lupe and to the Botten Then take the lupe and Pull over awala! a Butifole Butter fly. origami is my thing. After school I kurl in my Bed then take out my origami Book. But I do not turn on the TV because I need compleat consintroilon. I open the Book and Begin. I close my eyes the then POP! I start to read. Mw I fold the Bottem Left corner and the right. After going step by slep I finish. I got a warm felling called a complishment.

As I read I think what comes next? Aw . . . fold the top corner over the loop and to the bottom then take the loop and pull over. Voila! A beautiful butterfly! Origami is my thing. After school I curl in my bed then take out my origami book. But I do not turn on the TV because I need complete concentration. I open the book and begin. I close my eyes then POP! I start to read. I fold the bottom left corner and the right. After going step by step I finish. I get a warm feeling of accomplishment.

This is a page from Chris's writer's notebook so he's not concerned about mechanics. Like Ryan's piece about baseball, Chris has written about a beloved hobby. He does a great job of describing his complete engagement while he's making origami. There's a nice balance of externals (step-by-step motion) with internals (thoughts and feelings). The writing voice (Voila!) allows his childlike delight to shine through.

Chapter 8

Handwriting

Boys often have to attend so much to the physical process of writing that they have much less time to attend to ideas and meaning-making. They often become frustrated and completely lose motivation to write . . . One of my students, Alex, had this problem. He was a font of ideas, but it was so painful to watch him try to get them down on paper. I wrote an essay about him once, talking about how I feared he would snip off the end of his tongue because he had to concentrate so hard on guiding the pen. I wrote that his handwriting looked like "the footprints of wounded mice."

Doug Kaufmann

I chatted with a woman on a flight to Los Angeles.

"Can you guess what I do for a job?" she asked.

I had no idea. With a Flair pen she wrote her name on a paper napkin in lovely cursive.

"I'm a teacher." She pointed at what she had written. "You can usually tell a teacher because we were trained to keep the loops round and open when we write our *o*'s and *g*'s."

Handwriting issues have plagued me my entire life. My first-grade teacher, Mrs. Damon, solemnly explained this to me as a serious character defect—"You've got sloppy penmanship, and that means a sloppy personality." That sounds funny now, but at the time it really hurt. Mrs. Damon described my writing as "chicken scratching," and ordered me to write more neatly. She gave me nightly homework assignments to practice letters and words. Unfortunately all this practice did not smooth out my scrawling sentences, or make my writing any easier to read.

As a boy I was amazed and perplexed at the difference between the rickety writing of boys like me and the lovely letters that rolled smoothly and effortlessly from girls' pencils. Third and fourth grades marked the exciting transition from printing to cursive writing. Maybe things would be different in this brave new cursive world. Alas, I noticed the same disparity between boys' and girls' writing, even more pronounced. My handwriting still stank.

When I was a boy teachers made no distinction between substance (*what* you wrote) and appearance (how neatly you wrote it). Since handwriting *was* writing, my messy penmanship put me at the bottom of the barrel. This was a serious handicap I had to overcome in order to become a writer.

My handwriting never improved, but nowadays I write mostly on a computer, which makes it a nonissue. But many boys still struggle in school with this problem. At the beginning of my questionnaire I asked boys to complete the following sentence: "For me, the most enjoyable part of writing is . . ."

The results I received ranged from the most blunt and basic (". . . when it's done") to the rich and ruminative:

> Thinking what to write, and then it hits you.
> Just letting your thoughts flow onto the page.
> Reading it after you're finished.
> Relating to the characters.
> Letting other people feel and see my words.

Next I asked them to complete this sentence: "For me, the hardest part of writing is . . ."

I expected boys to reply by mentioning matters of skill and process, plus the sheer drudgery of writing: recopying, revising, getting mixed up, and having to fix all the spelling mistakes.

The first boy reported: "For me, the hardest part of writing is that my hand hurts."

The literalness of this response made me smile—I'm often taken aback by how concrete and tangible kids can be. On the next survey a fourth-grade boy wrote ". . . my hand gets sore." A third grader complained: "My fingers burn." One boy finished the sentence with a single word: "Handaches."

This was unexpected. Although it was not the most common response, a surprising number of boys reported that they experienced the act of writing as physically painful. No wonder their handwriting often looks messy or sloppy! If you asked girls to complete that sentence, I'm certain far fewer would have responded in this manner. This presents writing teachers with a basic dilemma: How can we get boys to love to write if they experience it as physically painful?

Most teachers I spoke to agreed that boys' handwriting suffers in comparison to the penmanship of girls.

"The first, most obvious thing I notice is that boys generally have a harder time writing neatly and quickly," notes Anne Hankins, a fifth-grade teacher at the Beijing International School in China. "Many boys comment that their hands hurt. It seems that the majority of the boys I work with have better large-motor coordination skills and weaker fine-motor coordination skills."

Is the notion that girls write more neatly in comparison to boys some kind of misleading educational fairy tale or urban legend? As it turns out, this widespread belief turns out to be true.

"There are exceptions, but here is the rule: Boys are graphologically challenged," says Christina Hoff Sommers (2004), author of *The War Against Boys: How Misguided Feminism Is Harming Our Young Men* (2001). Sommers quotes Steve Graham, a distinguished scholar and special education professor at the University of Maryland, who says, "That males have many more problems with penmanship than females is not even a question. It is one of the better established facts in the literature" (Sommers 2004).

"Many five-year-old boys just don't have the fine motor skills necessary to write the letters of the alphabet," Leonard Sax writes in *Why Gender Matters* (2005, pp. 94–95). He goes on to say: "Virginia Tech researchers found that boys are *years* behind girls in development of the area of the brain responsible for fine motor skills" (p. 95).

Does boys' poor handwriting negatively affect the way teachers respond to their writing? Let's consider a similar question: do adults lavish more positive attention, praise, or higher grades on a child who is more physically attractive than a less attractive child? No parent or teacher would be eager to admit this, yet several classroom studies have confirmed that this is true. Similarly, few teachers will acknowledge that they give more praise and higher grades to writing that has a crisp, easy-to-read appearance. Yet several studies have shown that this is the case.

"Illegible or poor handwriting can hinder students in getting fair and objective grades from their teachers," Pamela Farris reports in *Language Arts* (1991). "[T]he quality of students' handwriting influences how teachers evaluate papers; students with better handwriting receive higher grades than those with poor handwriting" (Sommers 2004).

Penmanship problems hamper boys' achievement in writing. But the problem is deeper than that. Issues of penmanship also hurt the degree to which boys get nurtured as writers. It doesn't merely affect how we formally evaluate and grade but also impacts a host of other intangibles: the emotional tenor of how we respond; the level of warmth in our voices; and the myriad subtle, nonverbal signals kids pick up during teacher-student interactions.

The teachers with whom I spoke had varying perspectives on this issue. Some lamented the fact that handwriting is no longer formally taught in most schools. Others were appalled that a surface feature like handwriting should so strongly influence, if not trump, our perception of more important issues of substance (theme, voice, and craft).

"Handwriting is not writing!" one teacher said angrily. "Anyone who feels that way should have their teaching license taken away!"

Maybe so, but I'm sympathetic to teachers who must trudge through countless pages of student writing. A typical middle school L.A. (language arts) teacher might easily read two hundred pages of student writing during a single week, often more.

"When I am collecting reading-writing notebooks (twenty-five each day every two weeks) I am reading six hundred to a thousand pages," Linda Rief told me. "That's all handwritten on smaller pages."

Writing with legible handwriting has a lovely transparency that invites us in; it gives us easy access to the world the writer is trying to create.

> On the other hand, poor penmanship acts as a
> fog or distorting filter that prevents readers from
> having full access to what has been written.
> Like a leaky faucet, or uncomfortable shoes a
> half size too tight, it creates an annoyance
> that is difficult to ignore. Word by word,
> sentance by sentance, paragraph by paragraph,
> it wears down even the most patient teacher.

"I've worked in many classrooms where the teacher is frustrated with the legibility of boys' writing and 'saves them for last' to conference with, and sometimes doesn't get to them," says Lori Lefkowitz, a reading specialist in Rochester, New York. "It's too bad because some of these boys have great seeds for writing."

What Can I Do in My Classroom?

Although there's no magic sword to slay this particular dragon, I'd like to offer a few suggestions for how to approach it, plus some ideas for how we might defuse the issue.

✘ Consider: how serious is the problem? Is the writing simply untidy or is it completely indecipherable?

"My first priority is that a child can read his or her own writing," says Suzanne Whaley. "If he can't, then that's an issue. When that happens it's worth intervening."

✘ Think: fluency. *Risk taking* and *fluency* are the main structural beams on which you build a strong writing classroom. By fluency I mean velocity: speed. Writing with velocity allows students' hands to keep pace with what's going on in their minds. It also helps them to outrun the censor most of us have in our heads. Solving the issue of handwriting is important not merely to create writing pieces that are easy on the eyes, but also so the student can achieve a level of sustained fluency.

✘ Make a distinction between the rough draft and final copy. Writing that will be read by an audience should have a clean, appealing look. Rough draft writing typically does look messy; there's nothing wrong with that per se. Try to be lenient with handwriting issues concerning boys' rough-draft writing. The penmanship is sufficient if the boy can read it to himself.

"When our thoughts are coming fast and furious, the quality of our handwriting spelling will naturally suffer," Frank Smith has written. "On the other hand, when we are concentrating on the correctness or appearance of the writing, the language will suffer."

✘ Type student writing. "One suggestion I make to teachers is to occasionally take a couple pieces from a boy and type them up," says Doug Kaufman, author of *Conferences and Conversations: Listening to the Literate Classroom*. "This may make reading for quality and structure of ideas easier."

Most teachers don't have time to type student work on a regular basis; still the strategy is worth considering, even if you do so only rarely. You can do this not only as a way to publish student writing but also in preparation for a writing conference. Typing student writing is exactly the kind of thing a parent volunteer could do to help out.

✘ Allow students to use the keyboard. When it comes to producing legible sentences, the keyboard is the great equalizer. Letters and words always look the same, no matter who happens to type them.

"Keyboarding is an essential life skill in this new millennium, whereas handwriting is not," argues Linda Silverman, author of *Upside-Down Brilliance: The Visual-Spatial Learner* (2002). "Some highly successful executives tell me the only use they have for handwriting is to write their names on checks. If the major issue in underachievement is handwritten assignments, and the solution is as simple as providing a child with a keyboard, what is preventing us from solving the problem?" (2006, p. 1).

Well, money, educators who work in poor districts might argue. This idea could open a new kind of Pandora's box—some kids don't know how to keyboard, many schools lack computers, and so on. And I do believe grasping crayons and markers serves the developmental needs for primary writers. But using a keyboard should certainly be an option for upper elementary stu-

dents. And this is happening. More and more I find myself
working in schools with students who are writing on inexpensive
laptops.

My teenage sons Robert and Joseph have handwriting that
can be hard to decipher. But when typing while IM-ing their
friends their writing comes fast and furious. Sure, there may be
spelling errors, but the writing is always perfectly legible.

✘ Talk about handwriting in ways that are descriptive, not pejorative. Given the research on boys' development, it's a mistake to
view poor handwriting as some kind of personality defect or
moral lapse (laziness). This problem should be viewed neutrally
as one area weakness in the context of other strengths and weaknesses. Some kids can't tumble very well; some have difficulty
with singing; others struggle with their handwriting.

✘ Don't take it personally. The boy whose handwriting resembles a
mane of wild, uncombed hair is not trying to make your life mis-
erable. Be compassionate. Remember: he's the one who suffers
the most from this problem.

✘ Don't lose track of the big picture. Sure, handwriting matters,
but it is really just a minor duke in the mighty kingdom of writing. That truth has been demonstrated again and again in the
real world.

Martin Toler Jr. was one of twelve men who perished in the West
Virginia coal miner disaster in early January 2006. Before Toler died
he scrawled a note in rough letters with an ink pen on a piece of paper,
signed JR. He wrote, "Tell all I see them on the other side. It wasn't
bad. I just went to sleep. I love you" (Figure 8–1).

The dead miner's final words were discussed by his nephew Randy
Toler, interviewed on CNN by phone from Tallmansville, a small
Appalachian mountain town where the mine is located.

"I think he wanted to set our minds at ease, that he didn't suffer,
and I just think that God gave him peace at the end," Randy Toler said.

Even as Martin Toler Jr. faced the end of his life, he clearly under-
stood his purpose as a writer. He imagined his family and friends who
would read his words. He knew that his words would make a difference in their lives. He wrote from the heart. And he didn't let a little
problem like messy handwriting get in his way.

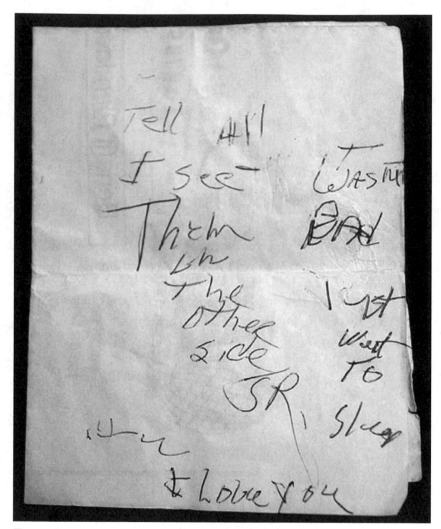

Figure 8–1

Missing Ahilet
Andres Vazquez, Grade 5

One day I was riding the bus home from school when I heard that an 8 year old girl got run over by an RV, as she was crossing the street with her mom and her sister, to school.

In YMCA, a girl sped in and said that a girl named Ahilet was run over. I couldn't believe that my cousin got run over.

On the day of the funeral, the birds were singing sadly. I went to touch her hand. It was cold like an ice cube had melted in her hand. Then I said to myself, I will never forget when Ahilet, her sister Lisette and I were laughing when my brother Miguel made a joke about my brother, Julio.

She's gone. I'll never see her again. No more tag. No more fun. No more laughing.

A family friend read a poem:

Mama don't cry for me.
I need to rest.

Twelve moons passed. We almost forgot her birthday. But, I remembered her birthday. I broke my piggy bank. I sent money to my aunt because they buried Ahilet in Mexico. My grandpa put a big bear that I won at the Chamarita on her gravesite. My dad had "I Love You, Ahilet" written on it. I saw this when I went to Mexico.

I'll never forget you Ahilet.

This piece of writing, a tribute to Andres's cousin, pretty much speaks for itself. The simple, short, declarative sentences in the next-to-last paragraphs are so powerful.

Chapter 9

Classroom Conversation

Although I hate to generalize about my students' behaviors, when I envision my classroom during book talk, I see girls waiting patiently to speak (I'm generalizing!) and being willing to "agree" with a peer, and build on ideas. I see Joe jumping out of his seat, looking for a space into which he can inject his idea. I hear John blurting out ideas, in the middle of Kelly's talk.

I do group boys together, but their discussions often seem like parallel play—they talk alongside and on top of each other!

Lynn Herschlein, fourth-grade teacher

What is a chapter on talk (conversation) doing in a book on writing? I include it here because in a healthy classroom, talk is the hidden glue that cements students' understandings while simultaneously bringing together the classroom community.

James Britton once wrote, "All that the children write, your response [as educator] to what they write, their response to each other, all this takes place afloat upon a sea of talk. Talk is what provides the links between you and them and what they write, between what they have written and each other" (1970, p. 29). I love this notion that reading is supported and buoyed up by the talk that is constantly flowing underneath it.

81

A few years ago I went into my son Robert's fifth-grade class. Over the course of six days I read aloud my book *Uncle Daddy*, an emotional novel about a boy whose father abandons the family for six years. The boy's life is thrown into turmoil when the father suddenly returns and tries to reestablish a relationship with his family.

I gave each student a notebook; every day after I finished reading I asked them to write a brief response to the chapters I'd read. Then we discussed the book. I was struck by the difference between the girls' and the boys' responses. The girls wrote long, thoughtful, ruminative entries. The boys' entries tended to be much shorter and more cryptic. But in the conversation it was different. The boys eagerly participated and made many strong points that were as profound as the comments girls made. The writing showed a discrepancy between the genders, but in the conversation the boys found a forum where they could match the girls.

Of the four language arts—speaking, listening, reading, and writing—speaking is a strong suit for most boys as well as girls. However, as we'll see in this chapter, boys typically employ a style of discussion that is different from that of girls.

Whole-Class Discussion

In 1992 the American Association of University Women (AAUW) released their famous report: *How Schools Shortchange Girls.* Among other findings, this report suggested that girls get silenced in the classroom, and lose self-esteem at adolescence. The AAUW Executive Summary said:

> *The educational system is not meeting girls' needs. Girls and boys enter school roughly equal in measured ability. Twelve years later, girls have fallen behind their male classmates in key areas such as higher-level mathematics and measures of self-esteem. Yet gender equity is still not a part of the national debate on educational reform. (p. 1)*

One of the key findings of the AAUW report came from the research of David and Myra Sadker, who suggested that teachers typically give boys more air time in classroom discussions. They reported that boys in one study of elementary and middle school students called out answers eight times more often than girls did. When boys called out, the typical teacher reaction was to listen to the comment. When girls called out, they were usually corrected with comments such as, "Please raise your hand if you want to speak."

This study received widespread attention in the press and fueled the ire of feminist theorists. Its blunt conclusions became accepted lore—teachers don't call on girls enough, and girls are suffering from it. Many teachers read this research and altered their teaching because of it. They made a conscious effort to call on girls more often in classroom discussion. (The Sadker findings have since been challenged by several researchers.)

In *You Just Don't Understand: Women and Men in Conversation* (2001), Deborah Tannen has described the conversational styles of men and women. She argues that whereas women often use talk to make or build relationships, men often use talk in a more competitive way, to establish a pecking order. Men talk about things; women talk about people. Men talk about facts; women talk about feelings. Men give information when they talk; women use talk to gain information.

Some of these differences may be exaggerated or oversimplified, but for now let's assume that there is some truth to the idea that males and females talk differently. If so, it makes sense that K–8 teachers, who are predominantly female, might favor the kind of "connected talk" in the classroom that women employ themselves. Such a discussion style would give girls an advantage over boys.

Brenda Power, my colleague and sometime editor, visited Franki Sibberson's fourth-grade class in Dublin, Ohio. The writing workshop began with a discussion about writing. Franki asked a question; kids who wanted to share a response raised their hands. Brenda told Franki that she was struck by the fact that Franki had called on eight boys in a row before she called on the first girl.

"Early in the year in four/five my work is often to win over the boys," Franki says. "I want to get them to trust me as a reader, trust that I know books, trust that learning will be good for them. So I have to work them hard—call on them, value their thoughts, and so on—a bit more than I do the girls at first because the girls in general often buy into reading more. If I don't have the 'cool boys' trusting the classroom and excited about the learning, it won't happen for everyone. So, I try to be inclusive and I have to validate the boys differently some years."

When I discussed this issue with Brenda Power, she said she noticed that Franki helped the boys to link their comments together.

"The girls are very comfortable with chaining on each other's ideas, and have mastered the niceties of jumping in at just the right moment with a comment connected to a peer's," Brenda noted. "Franki does more of the heavy lifting with boys in whole-class discussions—not just calling on them more often, but saying things like, 'Your comment reminds me of what Ben said a couple minutes ago about headings in the article . . .' She made explicit connections between ideas, teaching the boys how conversations work by providing those connections."

Franki Sibberson takes issue with any notion that girls and boys are forever stuck in gendered ways of conversing.

"I think boys do really well in an environment of connected talk," she says. "But they have to trust the environment. They have to know they won't fail. All kids need that but especially our struggling ones. My job for all kids, not just boys, is to create a space where they know they can try things out without failure."

When I visited the Boys Writing Club started by Jennifer Allen, a literacy specialist at the Albert S. Hall School in Waterville, Maine, and author of *Becoming a Literacy Leader: Supporting Learning and Change*, I had expected to sit quietly on the side and watch the boys interact with each other and with Jennifer. Wrong! The boys had read some of my books and, after the introductions, began to pump me for the inside scoop on writing and publishing.

"Where do you get your ideas?" Devin asked.

"Well, I—" I began.

"I read *Fig Pudding*," the boy immediately to my left interjected. "That was wicked good. But sad when that kid died."

I nodded. "I know. There are two really sad chapters. I wanted to end the book on an upbeat note."

"Yeah, when the kid steps in the fig pudding and they still eat it!"

"Endings are hard for me," another boy put in.

"How do you keep your grip on the reader?" a boy named Sam wanted to know.

"Wow, that's a great question!" I said.

"Yeah, I can write a good lead to hook my readers," Sam continued, "but how do you keep the readers interested until you get to the important part of the story?"

Before I had the chance to answer, another boy interrupted.

"You wrote *Flying Solo*, too, didn't you?" he asked. "Fact! Opinion! That was funny!"

For ten minutes it went like that, the boys loudly talking while they ate. There was such a spirited babble I could barely get a word in. Later Jennifer and I reflected on my first encounter with her kids.

"It was a great discussion about writing," Jen marveled. "But the kids kept talking over each other! They barely listened to what other kids were saying."

I had been thinking about classroom talk, and mentioned the idea that many girls showed an ease with connected talk. Boys, on the other hand, were less sensitive to what the previous person had just said and had a tendency to play their conversational card, no matter what had been said just before.

"That was it," Jen agreed. "Each boy was playing his card."

What Can I Do in My Classroom?

Classroom conversation is a key vehicle for creating a genuine feeling of community, where each student feels like he or she is a respected member whose voice is valued and listened to. Without that, the writing can't flourish.

✘ Assess the health of your classroom conversations. Do boys participate on a regular basis? Is one gender, with a prevalent conversational style, dominating the classroom?

✘ Make a point to actively engage the boys in classroom discussions, especially early in the year. Strive to create a safe environment where all kinds of ideas, responses, and conversational styles are welcome.

✘ Let kids choose their own small groups (with certain necessary exceptions). Don't be surprised if boys tend to group themselves with other boys; they may simply be finding the conversational style that best matches their own.

Next we'll look at the conversational structure that has the biggest impact on young writers—the writing conference.

AARON'S ADVICE LIFE
DON'T FEEL PRESSURED
Aaron Tyson, Grade 4

SOME PEOPLE JUST DON'T KNOW ME, BUT HEY, I KNOW ME. WHAT

EVER PEOPLE PUT AGAINST YOU LIKE A GRUDGE, YOU DON'T HAVE

TO

TAKE THE PRESSURE. YOU HAVE YOUR OWN LIFE AND IT'S GOOD,

REAL

GOOD. DON'T FEEL PRESSURED IN YOUR EVER BELOVED LIFE. LET IT

SHINE IN THE SUNLIGHT. DON'T FIGHT BE COOL, MATTER FACT BE

OVER

COOL, BE ICE COOL.

DON'T FEEL LEFT OUT JUST RELAX. DON'T LET JEALOUSY GET

IN YOUR HEAD, KILL YOU, MURDER YOU. JUST TAKE A DEEP BREATH

AND

SLOW THINGS DOWN. PLEASE TAKE MY ADVICE, NOBODY IS

PERFECTO OR FANTAZMAGARICAL. YEP! THAT'S RIGHT

FANTAZMAGARICAL!

YOUR LIFE IS ON THE LINE JUST LIKE A JAZZY FIZZLE. YOU JUST GOT

TO

KEEP THAT BEAT MOVIN. THEN IT WILL ALL END, IT WILL BE TIME,

FOR THE BIG CHOICE.

ALWAYS REMEMBER HAVE FAITH, WISDOM, KNOWLEDGE AND

UNDERSTANDING. WELL AT LEAST TRY TO HAVE UNDERSTANDING.

PLUS

REMEMBER ON EARTH EVERY SINGLE BODY IS A TERRIFIC,

FANTAZMAGARICAL ICE COOL WINNER. ALSO REMEMBER THINGS ARE

STRICT, BUT HEY! YO DON'T FEEL PRESSURED, DEEP BREATHS ALL THE

TIME, DON'T FEEL PRESSURED.

April 17 2006

Dear Ralph,

The don't feel presured poem is based on what true living lives are like today, and how I could at least try to help those living live. When I was little no older than 5 or 6 I didnot like writing or to even see a sheet of paper and a pencil together. Then when I got 6 I wrote stories Like, HOME Boy JACK, Cow, Harry Larry, and Timothy Tamblers all the way to 8. then I started poetry by the age of 9. EAch story I write helps me to get better and better. But Mrs. Leal dedicates me to write. But there is one new Story I'm going to Start called GAME. The GAME is about a kid named Gordon and how his Playstation Sparkles and Suddenly Gordon is in the GAME. Plus his friends are in the adventures. I wish I had time to stick around. Checkya Later!

Enjoy, Aaron Tyson

Aaron's piece is certainly unusual. I don't exactly know what genre I'd call this—part persuasive essay, part rap, part sermon. It's playful in tone and in language. And you can really feel Aaron's personality, his voice, shining through the words.

Chapter 10

Writing
Conferences

Most girls will naturally seek to affiliate with the teacher. They expect the teacher to be on their side, to be their ally. Most girls won't hesitate to ask the teacher for help when they need it . . . most boys will consult the teacher for help only as a last resort, after all the other options have been exhausted.

Leonard Sax, *Why Gender Matters*

O ne August I was running a summer workshop for about a hundred teachers at a school near Anchorage, Alaska. We were discussing ways to make writing conferences more effective. I wanted to model an actual writing conference, and decided to use myself as the guinea pig.

"I'm going to read aloud a piece of my own writing," I told the gathered teachers. "Then I'll invite anyone here to have a writing conference with me."

Primates
Sometimes as I hold or play with my infant son Robert, I'm struck by the realization that we are both primates. I'm a sort of ape, relatively intelligent, I hope, a clothes-wearing, book-reading sort of ape, but an ape nonetheless. A big ape taking care of a little one. See

how I groom him, nestle him, rock him when he starts to cry. If you stole into the room and watched me playing with him, I suspect it would be hard to distinguish the sounds we make—sighs, tribbles, grunts and murmurs—from the sounds made by any other primate male caring for his infant.

This piece was met with stony silence. I asked: "So, what would you say to me in a writing conference?"

More silence. I waited with what I hoped was a not-too-nervous smile. The piece I shared had come straight out of my writer's note-book, one of many pieces I wrote sharing my feelings and reflections on being a new father. Later, I put together a small, handmade book (*Overture: A Child's First Year*) that contained three dozen notebook snippets. I was hoping to demonstrate that uncovering the writer's purpose can dramatically shape the kind of response we give.

"Well?"

Finally, one teacher put up her hand.

"Why did you write about that?" she asked, frowning.

"I don't know." I shrugged. "I wrote it when Robert was a few months old. It just popped into my mind when I was holding him one day."

Another teacher raised her hand. She looked perplexed. "I guess I didn't get it. I mean, no offense, but after my son was born I never thought about him like he was an animal."

I nodded, trying not to feel defensive.

"Is this piece about evolution or something?" another teacher asked suspiciously. "Like humans are evolved from monkeys?"

"Not exactly," I replied. "But I guess having a new baby did make me feel connected to the animal world in a way I'd never felt before."

There was a long, uncomfortable pause.

"I kind of liked your comparison," one teacher finally offered. "It's a new way to look at it. It's different."

I glanced at her gratefully. But that comment was too little, too late. At that moment I felt neither lovable nor very capable as a writer. I felt angry, misunderstood, and a little silly. I felt those teachers' sus-picions toward me, almost as if I'd done something wrong. And I felt one other thing: a small, sharp splinter of shame.

Admittedly, that was not a realistic setting for a writing confer-ence. It was too public, there were too many people, and I had provided too little context for the teachers to confer effectively with me. But even so, I think there's something to be learned from it. The teachers in that room did not accept the particular slant I'd taken on my topic (baby as primate). Instead they had judged the writing. And, indirectly, they judged me.

Many boys experience something similar during a writing conference. They feel judged for what they choose to write about (topic), how they write about it (with wild action, slang, zany humor), and how the writing looks on the page (penmanship). Conferring well with boys requires new understandings, new skills, and a new openness to the passions boys reveal in their writing.

The Smell of Death

In Machiasport, Maine, a writing workshop was being run by Cyrene Wells, writing consultant and author of *Literacies Lost: When Students Move from a Progressive Middle School to a Traditional High School.* Cyrene approached an eighth grader for a writing conference.

"How's it going?" she asked him.

"I'm trying to describe the smell of death," he replied calmly. "But it's hard."

"The smell of . . . death?" Cyrene repeated, leaning toward him. She wanted to make sure she had heard him right.

The boy nodded. "It's a hunting story."

Cyrene was taken aback. She had never conferred about this topic.

"Let's you and me grab a piece of the floor," Cyrene suggested. "C'mon, let's talk."

The two of them moved away from the other students. They sat on the floor together, side by side, leaning against the wall. Cyrene listened as the boy explained what he was trying to write about. His story told about a time he and his father had gone on a hunting trip. The father shot a deer, and killed it. When the father took out his hunting knife and slit open the deer, a particular smell wafted into the air.

"It was the smell of death," the boy told Cyrene. "I want to describe what it smelled like, but it's hard. I don't know how to put it into words."

Cyrene nodded and paused. Not being a hunter herself, she didn't quite know what to say.

"It's important for my story," the boys said into her silence.

"I see that," she replied. "What can you tell me about the smell? Is it . . . terrible?"

The boy thought. "Well, it's not disgusting or anything. But it's pretty strong."

"Sometimes you can describe a thing by showing how it affects others nearby," Cyrene suggested.

"What do you mean?" he asked.

"By showing its impact on the people around it. How did this smell affect you and your father? How did you react? What did you do?"

The boy thought. "Well, when Dad cut open the deer, the smell came out. I didn't really do or say anything. Dad didn't say anything either. But he turned away. Dad never turns away."

Cyrene nodded. "That's important. If you describe your dad turning away, I think that will tell the reader a lot."

A pretty amazing conference, I think, and one that could easily have been derailed at the outset because of the adult subject matter. As soon as she heard what he was writing about, Cyrene could have made a face and said, "Please write about something else." She could have invoked school or classroom policy—no stories about guns, knives, hunting, killing, guts, gore—that would have ended this rich conversation and killed off the actual writing.

Cyrene brought several things to this conference. She brought an understanding of the culture in Downeast Maine, where deer hunting is an important tradition. ("Many boys I worked with have their richest experiences outside," she told me.) She recognized that the story was as much about an important father-son experience as it was about a slain deer. She accepted his topic in a neutral way, and helped him solve a problem he had diagnosed himself. In addition, she brought a writerly perspective—inside knowledge of craft— when she suggested he might show how the smell affected him and his father. This information was crucial to helping the student solve his writing problem.

We talk about the importance of giving students sufficient "wait time" after asking a question during a conference. In this writing conference Cyrene needed the patience to give *herself* adequate wait time so she could figure out how to proceed.

Conferring About Craft

I spoke with many teachers who acknowledged that they find it harder to confer with boys than with girls.

"In general my writing conferences tend to be most productive with girls because for one, I am a girl," admits Holly Martocci, a sixth-grade language arts teacher. "I feel that they sense I can relate better to them and their story/perspective than to the boys. Also, I find more girls willing to revise and 'perfect' their story than boys (who typically just want to get it done)."

I talked to other teachers who observed that boys don't seem to pick up craft elements as readily as girls do. We can introduce a strategy of craft element during a read-aloud or mini-lesson, and some kids (more often the girls) will run with it in their own work. It may be that boys need longer to incorporate it into their writing, and make the strategy part of their writing repertoire.

"The boys I teach seem to latch on to the descriptive elements of writing (exploding the moment, inner story, metaphoric language, etc.), but I have to conference with them about it first," says Todd Frimoth, a fifth-grade teacher in Vienna, Austria. "They kind of do it, but they don't do it naturally—it's more raw and unrefined."

I spoke to other teachers who agreed that the abstract nature of craft elements sometimes stymies boys, and leaves them unsure how to proceed. Those teachers tend to be more hands-on in a writing conference.

"My conferences with boys and girls do feel different," Lynn Herschlein, a fourth-grade teacher, says. "Girls seem to be more comfortable when I pose questions, turn them on to a mentor text, or leave them with more than one idea or possible direction. They respond and ask questions of me. These conferences take longer. Boys want to know, 'What should I do?' I ask, 'Well, what effect are you trying to create? or 'What do you think . . . ?' My questions sometimes frustrate them. I feel like they want concrete answers and direction from me. Sometimes I give in and say, 'You need a dramatic scene here.' Or 'Add some sensory details here.' They let out a sigh of relief, and I see in their faces, 'Okay, I can do that.'"

Our boy writers need to know that a craft element like creating character is not just some abstract idea but a useful tool that could enhance *this* story they are working on *right now*. The writing conference can be the ideal venue to help boys make this connection.

In a fourth-grade class I did a mini-lesson about using interior dialogue. As an example I read a section from *Uncle Daddy* where the reader gets to see what's going on inside the narrator's head while he's eating with his father at a restaurant. Afterward I conferred with Ethan, a tall red-haired boy who was working on a piece about a championship soccer game. The game ended in a tie; Ethan was the last to kick during the shoot-out.

"We just talked about interior dialogue," I said. "Do you think that might strengthen your story? Have you considered using it?"

He shrugged noncommittally.

"What was going on in your head when you took that last shot?" I asked.

Ethan closed his eyes, trying to remember. "I was nervous. I was trying to tell myself to stay calm."

"I bet! Do you ever talk to yourself when it's really tense like that?"

"Sometimes."

"At that moment what were you saying to yourself?"

He smiled. "Don't miss."

"Anything else?"

"Coach said the goalie was a righty. He said fake right, shoot left."

"Fake right, shoot left. Did you repeat that to yourself?"

"Yeah."

"This might be a good place to try some of that interior dialogue," I said, pointing to his story. "Right here when you're getting ready to shoot. Just write down the words you were saying to yourself: *Stay calm, Ethan . . . Fake right, shoot left.* Add anything else you were saying in your head. Try writing it first on a separate piece of paper. When you've done that, I'll show you how to include it into your story.

"Okay."

I started to get up, but then I sat down. "Hey, I'm dying to know. Did you score?"

"Yeah," he said. "My shot hit the inside of the post, but it went in."

Some boys may need a bit more hand-holding when it comes to incorporating craft elements into their writing. The writing conference is the perfect arena to give this extra support, to make the strategy concrete, tangible, relevant. Yet even with this one-on-one support boys may be indifferent or even hostile to our suggestions when it comes to revising their writing. In a second-grade class, Devin is furiously working on a cartoon with six boxes on a page. When JoAnn Portalupi goes to confer with him, he's eager to talk, and he's delighted with his work.

"Look!" Wide-eyed, he points at one box. "See what's happening? This character is breaking out of this box, and he's jumping down to *this* box! It's incredible! It's never been done in a comic book before!"

The story is a bewildering mix of fantasy, science fiction, and fighting, with a strong *Star Wars* influence. JoAnn makes a suggestion, but Devin ignores her and continues working. We have all worked with kids like Devin. These students tend to be male, and they pose particular problems in the writing conference. How do you help a young writer like that craft his story?

Jennifer Allen observed her son Ben as he wrote "Secrets of the *Titanic*." He wrote at home, and he spent many hours on the writing and drawing. I asked Jen if her son was receptive to her craft or revision suggestions when he was working on this story.

"No, Ben is never open to my ideas of revision," she said. "I have learned to leave him alone. Ben has probably ten different versions of his *Titanic* stories scattered around the house."

Many teachers find it frustrating to confer with boys like Ben and Devin. These boys seem hell-bent on writing their piece exactly as they want, complete with wild drawings, or talk bubbles, or whatever they feel like including. They don't seem receptive to, or even interested in, our revision suggestions. When conferring with such boys a teacher may feel ineffective at best, or a failure at worst.

"Boys (and some of my girls) have their own agenda and sometimes I feel I'm forcing too much of my 'crafting agenda' on them," says Ann Marie Corgill, a second-grade teacher at the Manhattan New School in New York City. "Sometimes I think that they're just developmentally not there for some of the lessons we present, and that's why they tune us out."

These writing conferences are not necessarily failures. Although we may not see tangible revisions, there may be a different payoff to those conferences. Writers like Devin and Ben are wholly engaged in writing about subjects they are passionate about. They give us a chance to validate a boy's independence, passion, and fluency. We get to find out what they know, and what they're deeply interested in.

To be clear: I believe that sometimes when conferring with boys we should back off and not push them to include a particular element of craft. If the boy doesn't want to revise, so be it. Now is the chance to celebrate and pay close attention to what the student is doing well.

"I can't wait to see the finished piece," you might say. Then just let them write.

"If they already have a way to write their piece, they may not immediately be willing to take on the craft idea we suggest," says Gayle Brand, a literacy teacher in Dublin, Ohio, and coauthor of *Practical Fluency: Classroom Perspectives, Grades K–6*. "But any time you conference about craft the boys do hear you. They pick up that thought and might use it in a future piece."

In order to do my best writing, I needed important conditions provided by my editors:

- ✶ They love my writing.
- ✶ They are wonderful readers.
- ✶ There's a give and take between my editors and me when it comes to revision. Even after discussing an issue, we don't always agree. When that happens we sometimes we end up doing it my way; other times we end up doing it my editor's way.

I wonder now: can we create these conditions for our boy writers?

- ✶ *Love their writing*. Well, maybe not the whole thing. But we need to find something to love in their writing: a section, a sentence, a telling detail, even one strong or unexpected word. We can savor it ourselves, and point it out to the student.
- ✶ *Be a wonderful reader*. We need to be skillful readers, bringing a rich understanding of the kinds of subjects boys like to write about, their peculiar humor, how they approach writing.
- ✶ *"Give and take."* To the extent that a teacher is willing to listen and accept the strong, strange, or unsettling elements in boys' writing (as Cyrene did), we show students our willingness to be flexible and meet them halfway.

What Can I Do in My Classroom?

- ✶ Don't be alarmed if your boys are less cooperative in writing conferences than your girls. And don't take it personally.

"A boy who is buddy-buddy with the teacher does not thereby raise his status in the eyes of his peers," notes Leonard Sax. "On the contrary, being friends with the teacher can *lower* a boy's status in the eyes of other boys" (Sax 2005, p. 85).

✘ Embrace a broader definition of writing. If we focus only on the writing on the page we may miss the most interesting stuff. Often the real writing may include drawing, talking, even gesticulating. These are ways that boys compose their story. In a writing conference we should pay attention and respond to them as well.

✘ In a conference, the strategies you suggest should be as concrete and tangible as possible.

✘ Give specific praise. Find a place to "plug in" to the boy's topic or his writing. Build on strengths. When you point out a strong element in a boy's writing, you're showing him that you're paying attention. Naming a strategy or craft element that a student has used will help him truly own it, and make it more likely he will use the strategy in future pieces of writing.

✘ Don't get into a power struggle over revisions. If the boy is engaged in his writing and resists revising, back off and let him write.

✘ Give more wait time in the writing conference. Many teachers commented on the fact that boys aren't as willing to talk about their writing, or as facile with doing so.

"This may be due to an initial reluctance to articulate a personally important idea," says Douglas Kaufman. "This probably holds true more for boys in upper elementary or middle school grades, who have been conditioned not to make themselves vulnerable. I sense that they often are weighing their words very carefully before they say them, and sometimes conclude that they shouldn't say them at all. They're thinking hard, though."

✘ Keep conferences short. Don't be too ambitious. Don't overstay your welcome. Less is better.

✘ Be aware of our body language and nonverbal signals. Many boys lack confidence as writers. During a writing conference they will be hyperaware, not merely of our words but also our subtle body language: the sighs, loaded silences, words inflected in such a way to reveal our frustration, suspicion, or outright disapproval.

The writing conference provides us with a rare, one-on-one opportunity to clearly signal to boy writers that we are on their side. Our unambiguous message to our boys must be:

I know that you can write well.
I believe in you as a writer.
I am genuinely interested in what you have to say, and how you write about it.

Memoir
Tyler Reeves, Grade 6

I hurled the strange, tiny, clam like creature that I called "pocket books" into the air and watched two seagulls fight over it. Then two more birds flew into the crowd. My friend, Clay, threw up another and a few more seagulls flapped into the blurry white mess of flying creatures. We began to run back to our section of the beach in front of our hotel while throwing more delicious pocket books over our shoulders. The white birds flapped after us. Then we jumped into our at least 5-foot deep hole with a splash. Even though it was far from the ocean, we dug the hole so deep there was water in it (once I found a fish swimming at the bottom of the hole. It must have been in one of the buckets of water that we threw in.)

Now there were dozens of seagulls flying around the hole, squawking for food. There was also a black pigeon with bright red eyes. He always hung out around the seagulls though he never attempted to eat a single pocket book (not that the seagulls actually ate the pocket books, they just caught them with their beaks and let them drop to the ground.)

We had almost thrown every pocket book in the bucket when we got some pretzels and cheese balls. Seagulls loved cheese balls. If we threw up a pocket book up only a few feet above our heads, they wouldn't go for it; it was too risky getting so close to humans. But with cheese balls, they did.

But there was one thing that the seagulls liked more than cheese balls: Bread.

My family had sub sandwiches for lunch. We ate by the beach. After we were finished eating, there were some scraps on the floor and some bread. There were also black olives since I hate them and took them all out of the sandwich. They loved bread so much, that once I held a piece in my hand and a bird got so tired of waiting for me to throw it that it swooped down and grabbed it, biting my finger in the process.

After every thing was gone, we decided to fish for the food.

Ally, Clay's sister was the only one who caught a single fish, and caught plenty of them. I think she caught ten in those 45 minutes, ten tiny shiny silver fish. We would throw them up live and the seagulls would catch them and gulp them down whole.

Ally may have been the only one who caught one, but we still all tried. We would get into the water (not too deep, for it was a red flag) and swoop our nets into the foamy, roaring wave.

Every day we devoted at least 30 minutes towards feeding the seagulls. They began to really love us and they were no longer afraid of us. We may not of been able to go in the water much, but that year's Destin trip was very special.

 This vacation story has an extra quality that makes it special. I love the strange detail (clams called "pocket books") in the lead sentence. There is a great deal of strong visual imagery in the story.

Chapter 11

A Dialogue with Carl Anderson

Carl Anderson is the author of several insightful books on writing, including *How's It Going? A Practical Guide to Conferring with Student Writers*. He and I had the following email conversation about working and conferring with boy writers.

RALPH: Before you were a staff developer you were a teacher. Do you think you tended to respond more favorably to boys or girls when you were a teacher?

CARL: When I think of my favorite students during the time that I was a classroom teacher (for eight years), most of them are girls. In part, I think this is because I had a rough time as a boy growing up. I wasn't athletic, I was smaller and quieter than other boys, I was a good student, I liked to read, I was more sensitive than other boys, etc. I was teased fairly often and quite cruelly by other boys throughout my elementary and middle school years. So as a teacher, when I encountered boys who embodied the qualities that I didn't have when I was a boy, I had trouble relating to them.

RALPH: In terms of writing did you notice any differences between your girls and boys? Who tended to be the strongest writers?

CARL: It's probably fair to say that when I was a teacher more of my strongest writers were girls. To be fair to the boys that I taught, however, I don't think that I created a classroom that was a place where many boys could imagine wanting to write, or wanting to become better writers. For example, I tended to discourage genres that boys enjoy (fantasy being one of them). I often shared mentor texts with the class that, as Tom Newkirk would say, violated the "boy code," i.e., ones that were very self-revealing and emotional in tone. And I didn't encourage students to write for purposes that many boys would value, such as to make your friends laugh out loud. In fact, I used to have a saying in my writing workshops: *No writing about blood, guts, aliens, or farting in writing workshop.* That one sentence probably turned off a good number of the boys I taught from wanting to write!

RALPH: Hmm. You are known for your thoughtful work on conferring with student writers. Do you think there are general differences in conferring with boys in contrast to conferring with girls?

CARL: There are a couple of ways to think of conferring with boys. One is with regards to boys' participation in conferences. Does it differ qualitatively with how girls participate? Honestly, in the classrooms I visit in which the teacher is an experienced writing workshop teacher, I don't see a vastly significant difference. In these classrooms, both girls and boys have learned to talk fluently about what they're doing as writers in my conversations with them, and take my suggestions for what I think they need to as writers seriously. While I certainly encounter boys who don't seem that engaged in their writing and who don't seem too keen to talk with me, this is true of some girls, too.

RALPH: Over the past ten or twelve years have you made changes in how you confer with boys?

CARL: Yes. What is different about conferring with boys now is how I respond to them. Over the years, I've learned to relate to boys better than I often did as a classroom teacher, and approach them in some ways that are different than I do with girls.

For example, I use humor to help them be more comfortable with me. I have a really goofy sense of humor, and I more often make a joke to start a conference with boys than I do with girls. I look for opportunities to make male-to-male connections with boys, too. When a boy comes up wearing a sports jersey or a T-shirt with the name of a music group on it, for example, I usually make some comment that indicates that "I'm in the club." (I wasn't athletic, but I did develop a very healthy interest in most sports, except football. Although I rarely watch sports on TV, I'm an avid reader of the sports pages, in part because I enjoy the stories, but also because I know that I can weave talk about current sports news into conferences.)

RALPH: Do you think being a guy makes you more sympathetic to boy writers? Does it help you relate to them better, or help them relate to you?

CARL: Yes, of course it helps that I am genuinely in the boy club in the biological sense. The boys with whom I confer today have no idea that I was once the kind of boy they would probably have teased! Especially in elementary schools, where male teachers are few and far between, I think that many of the boys I confer with today are excited to talk with a man.

RALPH: How else have your boy writing conferences changed?

CARL: I've learned to become more genuinely interested in certain topics that boys enjoy writing about—video games, for example. For many years, I was against boys writing about video games. Why this should be true is beyond me, since I spent many hours of my sophomore year at Duke obsessively playing Space Invaders! Now I welcome the challenge of helping boys write well about video games. Narratives about video-game playing, I've come to believe, are stories either of personal triumph (I've conquered Level 12!) or companionship or rivalry with another boy.

RALPH: You've touched on a major point of frustration for many teachers. How *do* you confer with a boy when he's writing about a video game?

CARL: The trick of conferring around this topic, I think, is helping boys get themselves into the stories, instead of just describing what happens on each level of the game. And if they want to write about the games themselves, I've learned to nudge them toward writing feature articles, reviews, or how-tos as a means of writing about them purposefully and well.

I've noticed that many women teachers discourage video games as a topic. I think this is because many of them didn't have my Space Invaders experience. This fall, I was coaching a teacher who was conferring with a third-grade boy who was writing about video games. Her frustration at the child's choice of topic was pretty evident to me throughout the conference. And she really had no idea of how to help the boy write his story effectively.

When the conference was over, part of my advice for her was to borrow a Game Boy and play a few games herself. She wouldn't have as much trouble helping boys envision how to write about video-game playing when she conferred, I explained, if she drew upon her own experience with playing one.

RALPH: How do you confer with a boy when his writing contains "boy humor," which can sometimes be crude?

CARL: Well, I've had to learn to become more comfortable with the kinds of bodily functions that boys love to include in their writing. For example, I've come to appreciate the value that boys place on writing about throwing up or farting in their stories. In January, I was conferring with a second-grade boy at PS 321 in Brooklyn, in front of a group of teachers who were almost all women. The boy had written a story about a boy who had had a falling-out with his best friend. How did the main character solve this problem? In the final scene, the main character is kind of glowering at his former best friend. Then, one of them farts, causing the other to laugh. Then the other one farts, causing the other to laugh. All of a sudden, the two boys are friends again!

RALPH: [*laughing*] Ah, the ultimate male bonding experience!

CARL: Yes! I remember when I was reading the story in the conference (out loud so the teachers could hear it) and I got to that final scene. The author tensed up a little when I started reading about the farting, probably expecting that I would be upset with him. But I just laughed and told him that I thought he had found a great way to end his story. I said that because I remember the absolute delight I once had as a boy with farting around my friends, and because I could absolutely see how two boys farting could break the ice between them. Earlier in my career, I would have shut this kind of story right down, and told the author that it didn't belong in writing workshop. I've changed my mind, ultimately because I've come to believe that shutting these kinds of stories down gives boys the message that they should submerge part of their identities as boys in writing workshop. And for some boys, that's too big a price to pay for being part of the community, so they quite understandably lose interest in writing in school.

RALPH: Complete this sentence: "What teachers don't understand about boy writers is . . ."

CARL: One thing that teachers don't fully understand/appreciate about boy writers is . . . what it is to be a boy. I think that some boys in writing workshops feel like the title character in David Shannon's very wonderful picture book *No, David!* who constantly gets in trouble for doing all the fairly typical things that many boys do. Imagine that book set in writing workshop. No, David, don't write about video games! No, David, no more characters burping in your stories! No, David, no more making fun of things in your writing!

RALPH: What happens to boys who don't connect to the kind of writing we have them do in school?

CARL: Many boys who don't feel valued as boys in school develop a secret writing life. It's interesting to read about John Lennon's life as a schoolboy. He wrote a little newspaper for his friends full of parody and wicked wordplay and weird drawings. Of course, this writing wasn't valued by his teachers (many of whom saw him as a nasty rebel who was destined to be a failure in life!). John's story is a good example of how one boy had to go underground with his literary interests because they weren't appreciated in school.

As a teenager, I also had a secret writing life. Outside of school, I wrote poems and plays that I kept hidden behind the pile of *Mad* magazines that I stored in a drawer in my desk (hidden away from the eyes of my mom and two sisters!). How I wish that my teachers at the time were interested in the kinds of writing I passionately cared about during those years and the topics I explored in my writing. In school, however, we only wrote literary essays about books that I had trouble understanding or caring about very much. So, like John Lennon, I went underground.

It's my hope for boys in writing workshops today that we revel in the topics they want to write about, and the genres they want to write in. I hope that boys don't feel the need to go underground with their writing lives, or to shut down as writers entirely. Instead, I hope they feel that writing workshop is a safe place for them to write about what matters to them, and make sense of their lives.

A Season to Remember

Alden Quimby, Grade 8

This year in the NHL was definitely one of the most memorable in a long time. This is the first year in the history of the NHL that every single goalie had a Goals Against Average (GAA) of 0.00 and no players scored any goals. Not even one. Oops, maybe I forgot to mention the fact that the NHL didn't happen this year, and that is was officially cancelled a few weeks ago, when Gary Bettman, the commissioner of the league, announced that the players association couldn't come to an agreement with the NHL about the salary cap limit.

At the point of the cancellation, there had been a total of 155 days missed because of the lockout, and there had been 1,161 games cancelled. During that time, the average person would have taken 3,100,000 breaths, slept for 1,300 hours, watched 600 hours of television and gone #2 about 150 times. Personally, I think the league should have been cancelled a long time ago, right around the 20th trip to the john. After canceling over 100 games, I gave up all hope and decided that the NHL had absolutely no chance of making it.

But seriously, let's take a minute to stop and figure out what these people are having such a grueling debate about. The NHL proposed a rejected salary cap of $44.7 million. If the money was distributed evenly throughout the team, each player would earn somewhere in the area of 1.9 million dollars a year. 1.9 MILLION dollars! I would die for a salary like that. I'd be blowin' my nose in Benjamin's and wipin' my butt with Grant's if I was rakin' in that kind of dough! (That'd be pretty sweet, huh?) Anyways, after the players rejected that offer, they suggested a $49 million cap. With $49 million per team, each player would get about $2.1 million. Wait, what! This entire debate has been over 0.2 million dollars! Wow!

Well, at least we Americans can say that the athletes of our era aren't getting greedy of anything like that. I mean, that would be just so horrible if they were so greedy as to not play for an entire year because they want $0.2 million more on their contracts. The average player makes around $2 million. So it's great that our athletes are mature enough to play hockey instead of argue over the measly sum of $200,000. I mean, $200,000 dollars is only like the total salary of 5 Americans in one year. But that's nothing to the pro hockey players of our day. Adding $200,000 to their salary is only adding 10% to the total. Basically, 10% of a pro hockey player's salary is worth as much as the salary of five Americans. Gee, I sure am glad there's not a massive debate over that kind of money!

I can't wait until I get older, and I have a chance to pursue my hockey career by joining the players' association. Maybe by the time I'm there, we can debate over $250,000 when each player is making about $8 million a year. That'd be great! And then everyone in the US would think so highly of me, and I'd be a star!

Pssh! Who am I kidding!? The NHL is a joke! This year has probably been the most pathetic year in the history of our sports. The athletes are getting so amazingly greedy that the entire Great Wall of China would be needed to stop the landslide of greed our athletes created. If I, or any of my children, grow up to be great athletes, I'll definitely make sure that our minimum salary is $20 mil and I wouldn't stand for anything less. I mean, that's not greedy or anything, is it?

RF

This is a piece of sports commentary. After studying Rick Reilly, Alden shows he can "talk the talk." He has written a piece that contains the biting sarcasm and irreverent perspective of a veteran sportswriter. I love the lead paragraph. The inclusion of so many numerical figures seems appropriate for the subject matter (athletes' skyrocketing salaries). (Alden's writing piece also appeared in the following publication: Rief, Linda. 2006. "What's Right with Writing." Voices from the Middle *13 (4): 32–39.)*

Chapter 12

Sticks and Stones: Language Issues

When we use certain phrases . . . we run the risk of being judgmental (or at least viewed that way by the kids). Judging boys in this way will limit our ability to teach the child. Children easily detect people being judgmental, and it means that they are no longer safe to explore. Judgment stands in the way of the relationship between teacher and student, and teaching is nothing if not relational.

Peter H. Johnston

As a young freelance writer I submitted a short story to a magazine. One month later I received a form rejection note. Undaunted, I sent five of my poems to the same magazine. This time the editor sent back my poems with a handwritten note: "Bad, bad, compares with your prose." Even now after publishing thirty-five books, those six words still sting.

Language can deeply wound, and leave lasting scars. On the other hand, the words we speak can be crucial missing ingredients to help a kid make a breakthrough in his writing.

When you think about it, much of the language that gets used in school is downright *weird*. Schools contain a specialized jargon, words and initialisms that label kids with learning problems or "special needs": ADD, OCD, LD, ELL . . . Far more boys are coded in this manner than girls (see Appendix B). In school many boys find themselves pinned, wriggling, by a coded diagnosis. It's true that these labels can act as a catalyst for much-needed individual help, but many boys feel stigmatized by these labels.

Note that we don't say: He *has* ADD. More typically we say: He *is* ADD. He *is* OCD. (The same thing is often true for writing assessments. It's not: He *scored* a 2. It's: He *is* a 2. She *is* a 4.) One of the dangers of such labels is that they lead us to see the student as fixed or permanent instead of growing and changing. In such a context it's a challenge to see boy writers through a clear lens, particularly when the language they use often seems so alien to our own.

Boy Language

A friend of mine found her two-year-old sitting on the little plastic potty late one morning.

"But you already went poops," she said.

"I know, but I'm crapticing," he explained.

Everybody has language stories about very young boys, anecdotes that never fail to make us giggle and laugh. It's telling that we rarely tell similar stories about older boys, maybe because the way they use language isn't always so cute and endearing. Boys often speak and write with language that can seem "fresh" (in the negative sense), rude, smart-alecky, vulgar to adult ears—words that once prompted mothers to wash out their kids' mouths with soap. Boys have various reasons for using such language: for fun, to defy authority, to express solidarity with peers, to make an individual mark, or maybe just to experiment. Certainly popular culture has a huge impact on the language boys use when they write.

My son Robert likes reggae. Joseph likes hard rock (AC/DC, Pearl Jam, Led Zepplin). Both boys listen to rap artists like Michael Franti, Sublime, Hieroglyphics, Deltron, Gangstar, KRS-One. Much has been written about the violence and sexually explicit nature of rap lyrics. I know it appeals to boys in general; still, I wanted to understand why it appealed to *my* boys in particular. What did they see in it? I've been letting them play rap songs while we're driving. (If a song includes too many F-bombs, I get to switch to the next one.) These rap lyrics run the whole gamut—clichéd, clever, funny—and some are shocking.

But shock, of course, is the point. I have to remind myself that every generation finds lyrics, language, and slogans that resonate with its spirit, that define it as new and different from what came before. Today high schools across the country hire DJs for school proms and insist those DJs play sanitized versions of popular songs. But students find a way to get around it. At exactly the right time the students—even the "good kids," who never get in trouble—defiantly yell out the curse words that have been omitted.

In school I was one of those good kids (altar boy, Eagle Scout), yet I vividly remember my first dance in seventh grade. I was on the dance floor when the DJ played Bob Dylan's "Rainy Day Women # 12 & 35," and I joined everybody else in shouting, "Everybody must get stoned!" even though I realize now I didn't have a clue what "getting stoned" really meant.

Language issues instantly arise when we read boys' writing and must make a snap judgment about what's acceptable and what is not:

Our team sucked.

The test pissed me off.

My cousin has a new girlfriend but he says he isn't getting paid yet.

Ideally, writing teachers should become knowledgeable about the pop expressions and slang boys use in their writing. Often our alarm at the language in a boy's writing says more about us than it does about him because we don't understand what a word or expression means.

"That hill is sick," Joseph said while skiing one day.

"You didn't like it?" I asked.

He rolled his eyes at me. "Dad, sick means, like, good."

Another time he said, "Chris's lacrosse gloves are *nasty*."

I gave him a puzzled look.

"Nasty means really cool," he explained.

"I thought nasty was bad," I told him. "I've heard you say, 'These french fries are nasty.'"

"It can mean either one," he said impatiently. "It depends on how you say it."

With boys' language, as with their humor, we should acknowledge the limits of our understanding and try to learn exactly what is being said. Language is a restless tide—ever shifting, changing, ebbing, and flowing. To me the word *pimp* is linked to prostitution and therefore distasteful. But kids who watch a popular TV show see it as a hip new word, a verb that means simply "to fix something up and make it look fancy." When Ellen DeGeneres remarked on TV that she planned to "pimp" a friend's baby carriage the soccer moms in the studio audience laughed heartily.

I remember coming home for a holiday as a twenty-year-old. At the dinner table I told a story in which I said, "I was really pissed off—"

"Don't you *dare* use that language around here!" my father shouted.

Stunned, I stopped. I hadn't meant to be offensive. Looking back now it's clear that in 1972 the phrase *pissed off* had not yet worked its way into the mainstream. To my father's ear those two words must have sounded like a vile curse.

Fifteen years later, while eating with my family at a restaurant, my father told a story and said, "My brother John got one letter that really pissed him off . . ." I smiled to myself, feeling vindicated. But I realized he was not being hypocritical. Times had changed. That phrase had become accepted into the culture so that even "nice people" could say it in mixed company.

But I think back to that first *pissed off*, when I got reprimanded for using that phrase. I felt judged, rebuked, cut off from the language I would naturally have used. So I simply shut up for the rest of that meal.

Teacher-to-Teacher Language

A teacher told me the following story:

"At the beginning of the year I had one boy, Juan, who was really struggling with his writing. During the first few workshops he just sat there and produced almost nothing. I ran into the teacher Juan had had the previous year, and shared my concerns about his writing. The teacher just shook her head.

"'Don't even bother,' she said."

Some might describe such a comment as negative but essentially harmless since it was spoken between two teachers in a private conversations. I would argue that even if the student never hears that comment it will ripple out through the school and hurt his development as a writer.

In my survey I asked teachers to react to this statement about boy writers and audience: "Most girls write for the teacher; boys write to entertain other boys."

About 80 percent of my respondents said that they thought this was true. One teacher who agreed added this: "It's true that boys tend to write to entertain. But I still think that if we teach, model, and practice, boys abandon this grandstanding opportunity."

Let's consider that word: *grandstanding.* The dictionary defines grandstanding as "performing ostentatiously so as to impress an audience." I looked up synonyms: *ham, impress, show off, attract attention, showboat.* Grandstanding is a negative way to describe something (knowing and connecting with his audience) that could have been described as a real strength.

Consciously or unconsciously, we may fall into the habit of using language that is charged and negative when talking with colleagues about writers and their writing. For instance, I often hear teachers say that they don't want boys to glorify violence. Like the word *grandstanding, glorify* is a "ramp-up" word. Boys don't *use violence* or *include violence* or *experiment with violence* in their stories—they *glorify violence.* That verb pushes violence up another notch or two to emphasize just how unpleasant it is.

Many of us may use ramp-up words or expressions without being aware of it. For example, some teachers told me they don't like it when boys put "gratuitous violence" in their stories.

"Interesting that we never talk about 'gratuitous dialogue,'" observes Peter Johnston.

What bothers me about such language is that it is *pejorative* rather than *descriptive.* If I were a lawyer defending the boys I'd want to leap out of my chair and shout: "Objection! Argumentative!" Words and phrases like these contain an implicit judgment—the kid is guilty simply by the words we use to describe the writing.

Teacher-to-teacher talk may seem tangential to the real issues facing boy writers, but I believe it has a lot more impact than we think.

"Some people think you transform schools by putting students in uniforms, others by simply flooding classrooms with books," Shelley Harwayne says. "For me the real way is to watch our language, being careful of how we talk to and about the students, their parents, and our colleagues." In her book *Going Public,* Shelley suggests that teachers "imagine that everything they say to their students is somehow broadcast throughout the entire building on a public-address system" (1999, p. 122).

Teacher-to-Student Language

A close friend of mine took a writing course while she was in grad school. All her papers came back with a B- grade. When she met with the teacher he told her: "You've got good ideas, but you've got sentence-level problems."

"That wasn't very helpful," my friend said with a frustrated sigh. "It's like someone telling you: 'You seem like a nice person but I can't stand your personality.' What do you do with response like that?"

A teacher's response to a writer carries a great deal of weight. We should never forget that when we make our suggestions or comments. In my survey I asked boys if they ever remembered being criticized for their writing. One boy responded, "In second grade my teacher said my writing was worse than kindergarten."

Another boy remembered, "My first-grade teacher said my writing was pitiful. I still don't like to write."

Pitiful is a barbed word, a painful splinter not easily removed from a kid's psyche. A destructive remark like that can create lasting damage to a boy's self-confidence and passion for writing. It won't take long for a boy who hears comments like that to internalize the message that *writing is one of those things I'm not good at and probably never will be.*

On the other hand, many kids reported that at least one teacher had given them praise—also words they never forgot.

> She said my lead made a movie that she could see in her head.
> She said she read my poem to her husband and they both
>   laughed.
> My teacher liked the way I made a circle story.
> He said my camping story sounded like a Gary Paulsen book.

Careful, specific praise—where the teacher names something the student did in his or her writing—will fuel a young writer for a long time. Boys may seem stoic, aloof, indifferent to what a teacher says about their writing, but that's misleading. Every boy needs to hear praise, even if we cite only one part of his story, one sentence, one word!

I visited one school where a teacher told me, "In our school, when we confer with kids we try to give them a glow and a grow—something they're doing well, and something they need to work on." I like this idea because it reminds us that both are necessary in order for a young writer to flourish.

What Can I Do in My Classroom?

As teachers we should be more accepting with the edgy language boys employ in their writing, even those phrases that test the limits of what we deem acceptable. At the same time we need to be more careful with our language when talking to them or even about them.

✖ Take the hot air out of ramped-up words and expressions. Use language that is neutral and descriptive instead of judgmental when talking to kids about their writing.

✖ Be flexible when students use slang and popular expressions in their writing.

✖ Take a firm stance against students who make sarcastic put-downs of other students during writing. You simply cannot allow it.

✖ Look for positive ways of describing boy writing, both when speaking to students and about them to peers. Instead of, "Oh, he's always grandstanding" you might say, "He sure does know his audience. He's skilled at writing the kinds of stories and poems that connect with other boys in the class."

✖ Beware of making derogatory comments that may inflict lasting damage. We don't need to warily "walk on eggshells" around our boys, or sugarcoat our language when speaking with them. ("I'm a rather direct, blunt, tough-love conferrer," Isoke Nia says, "and I have grand conferences with the boys.") But spoken words, which seem to dissolve harmlessly into the air, really can leave a lasting impression. Every writing teacher should remember the physician's creed: first, do no harm.

The Majestic Moose
Oliver Leckenby, Grade 3

A ray of light faltered over a very grimy house. Al Rat opened his
one window. He moved over to this desk, shooed away his five
rats, and started to grade school papers. He wrote "Ugh!" on one
and giggled.

Genesee Park, 1975 – A school bus pulled up a narrow road
and stopped. Genessee Park is very rich with predators. There are
a lot of old homes and there are a lot of diamonds in the ground.

The door opened and one kid after another flew out of it. One
last kid flew out the door. Out stepped a grizzly Mr. Rat.

Mr. Rat chained the children's arms to their sides and prodded
them forward with one of his bone spears (the kids suspected they
are human). First he brandished a snake he whipped from his
pocket.

"It's poisonous!" Mr. Rat said.

"Is not," said a kid.

"Not?" Mr. Rat said, almost whispering. All in a split second,
the snake flew at him taking a big chunk of his nose. Mr. Rat
yanked the snake off his nose and snarled, "May that be lesson to
all you freaks."

He led them to the forest. They got tossed in a clearing that
had a big cave in the middle of it. With a rumble, a bear erupted
out of the cave like a big furry torpedo.

"Bears are carnivorous," Mr. Rat said coolly. The bear jumped
headlong into the kids.

Mr. Rat stepped out of the way as the bear ate his way
through the yelling kids. It was total commotion.

Mr. Rat chortled with amazing vigor. (After all the bear got a
stomach-ache from eating too much.) He led the five remaining
kids to a cliff.

Suddenly, the underbrush exploded and a moose barreled out
of nowhere. It hit Mr. Rat and the two of them fell and fell.
Thump!

The End

(or is it?)

Bonus Chapter Two

Mr. Rat burned in the fiery pits from that day on.

RF *What a wild story! Yes, it does contain violence and that alarmed me at first until I realized that the whole thing is a put-on. My boys found it wickedly funny, though adults may not recognize the humor at first (like those cell phone ring tones that only teenagers can hear). Oliver uses lots of odd details (diamonds on the ground). Some of his verb choices are absolutely stunning (brandished, chortled).*

Chapter 13

Drawn to the Page

My boy writers tend to spend lots of time on the detail of their pieces—whether it's the sharp animal teeth, the thousand different parts on a robot, the extra gadgets on their tanks or helicopters, lots of smoke and flames in their explosions, etc. On the whole the girls balance writing with illustrating, but my boys are heavy on the illustrating.

Ann Marie Corgill, second-grade teacher

For the past five years Martha Horn and Mary Ellen Giacobbe have been working with kindergartners in Boston public schools. When they describe their work I am struck by their talk about drawing. They spend lots of time showing kids the illustrations in picture books. In mini-lessons they model for kids how to draw those pictures, and give kids explicit instruction in how students can make the drawings themselves.

Many educators would agree that drawing serves the developmental needs of primary children. Here I'd like to put forth the more radical idea that upper-grade boys, too, would greatly benefit from drawing as part of their composing process.

When I wrote my memoir (*Marshfield Dreams: When I Was a Kid*) I started by sketching a rough map of Acorn Street, the neighborhood **119** where I grew up in Marshfield, Massachusetts. I penciled in the swamps, streams, woods, and large granite boulders, plus the Unexplored Territory we weren't allowed to explore. Recently I shared this map with a group of sixth graders and invited them to draw their own neighborhood maps.

The kids went to it. The boys in particular really seemed to relish the chance to construct those maps. It was as if they were being invited to play an old, beloved game. Kids sketched forts, traps, tree houses, graves of buried pets. One boy added a special insert that was a blowup of his cellar. Another invented a special legend as Jerry Spinelli did in his map at the beginning of his memoir, *Knots in My Yo-yo String*. I asked the kids to mark an *X* plus a word or two to indicate where something had happened, a spot where a story might be buried. I also asked them to put a *D* for any danger spots. Those neighborhood maps eventually led to some marvelous writing.

Other writers have found that making a map of a place, real or imaginary, can act as a springboard for a writer's imagination. Claire Harman is the author of *Myself and the Other Fellow: A Life of Robert Louis Stevenson* (2005a). In an interview aired on NPR's *Morning Edition Sunday* on November 27, 2005, Harman talked about how Stevenson created an imaginary map that sparked his imagination and led to the creation of his most famous book.

"Well, they were on a wet holiday in Scotland and most holidays in Scotland are wet holidays, and they got stuck indoors with nothing to do," she said. "And Sam [Stevenson's son], who was twelve years old at the time, had a paint box and some paper. And Stevenson, having painted a map of an island, then became absolutely entranced with his own picture. And, you know, his imagination just flooded into this picture of an island and . . . to him it suggested a whole story about pirates and adventure and the period which he loved, which was the . . . early to mid-eighteenth century. Everything seemed to fall into place, and having painted the painting, he then immediately set about writing the first chapter of *Treasure Island*. And he wrote a chapter a day while the rain kept going. If the weather had been better that August in Scotland he might well never have written the story" (Harman 2005b).

Left to their own devices boys love to include drawings in their stories. (See Figures 13–1, 13–2, and 13–3.) If you take these drawings seriously and study them you'll see that they typically contain a great detail of information: important details, characterization, plot, a

chaPterj P,mk,n lm,n

Pumkin mam
unde a Grave in Blackmoon
Grove yard lived a Pumkin in
a Golish house (Manchen)
And There what villen Ritten
all over him.

FIGURE 13–1A PAGES FROM THE STORY "THE PUMPKIN MAN," BY JOSEPH FLETCHER.

sense of place. You find passion and humor in boys' drawings. You find *voice*.

"Drawing is something all boys like to do," says Arthur Voigt, a literacy consultant in New York. "There are at least three or four other things they should all draw: a map of their neighborhood, a self-portrait, a drawing of what they see in their dreams, a picture of where they see themselves in ten years, a picture of their favorite hero, and so forth."

Unfortunately, teachers in most classrooms don't see drawing as an activity with much intrinsic value during writing time. Instead,

FIGURE 13–1B

drawing is viewed warily as something kids get away with, like chewing gum or listening to an iPod on the sly.

In upper-grade classrooms boys may be allowed to draw from time to time, but opportunities are limited. The teachers who do allow students to draw impose rigid limitations—only in pencil, and only for a little while. Some teachers allow students to "sketch to stretch" as a reading comprehension strategy. (This strategy first appeared in *Creating Classrooms for Authors and Inquirers* [Short, Harste, and Burke 1995]. After reading a text, students create a sketch depicting their interpretation of the text or events in a book.) And teachers may allow boys to create illustrations to enhance their published work.

the Battle lasted 30 Years.
But on one stormy Day The Last
ov servivers wer Finished
and the wav ended.
The Knight Crawled up from
The Ground. As he
lookid across the Grounds he
Relised that the Battle
had ended.

<small>Figure 13–1c</small>

"The boys are delighted each month when they get to spend some time illustrating their published work," notes Valerie Collins, a teacher in Denver, Colorado.

That's fine. But what about the drawing boys might do not only at the end of the process (publishing) but as a part of the composing itself?

When third grader Ben Allen wrote "Secrets of the *Titanic*" (p. 95) he included drawings to convey important historical facts. Jennifer Allen believes that making these elaborate illustrations helped her son think through the topic he was writing about.

"I think Ben is processing ideas while he's drawing," she says. "He has been drawing pictures of Johnny Damon (with notations that these

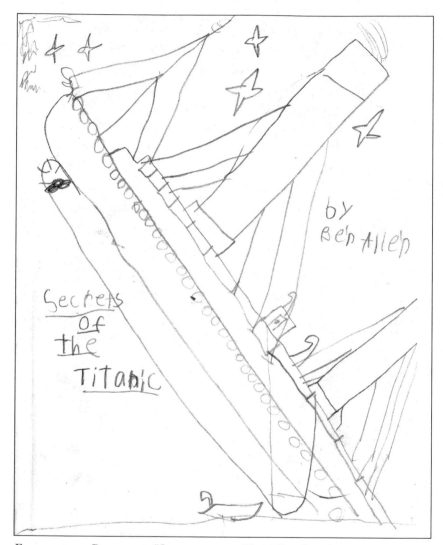

FIGURE 13–2A PAGES FROM "SECRETS OF THE *Titanic*," BY BEN ALLEN.

are of him before he left the Red Sox) over the last few weeks. Then out of the blue yesterday, he went outside and wrote this piece on the history of the Boston Red Sox, no illustrations, just text. It's like he finally put his pen to paper and wrote what he had been thinking about for the last few weeks. I think for Ben there is a strong connection between the need to draw and then write. I am not sure he is given these opportunities in school."

This idea is supported by recent brain research. Writers like Michael Gurian (2005b) and Leonard Sax (2005) point out that girls'

The biggest ship in the world

year 1912

Titanic is being robled in to the wateh. Titanic is the biggest ship in the world. It has a post office, swimming pool and a restorant. The Titanic is 11 stohes7all and it is up Eityblocks long. Titanic is taking its fist

FIGURE 13–2B

brains are wired for language: words. This contrasts with boys' brains, where more cortical areas are devoted to spatial-mechanical functioning. It would make sense, then, that allowing boys to draw as part of their writing process would play to their strength in that spatial area.

"The elementary classroom is four-fifths language based, and so the girls have a huge advantage there," says Gurian (2005a, p. B1). He suggests that drawing a subject first can help many boys write better about it.

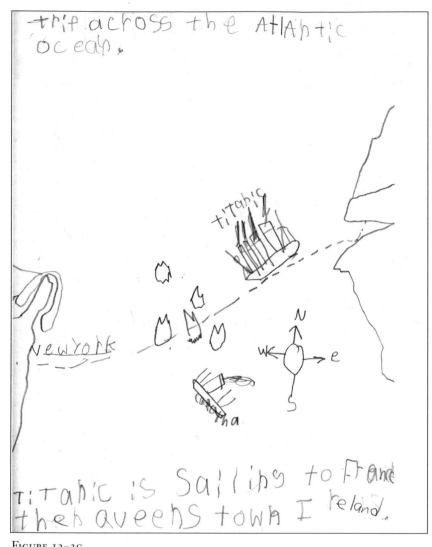

trip across the Atlantic ocean.

titanic

New york

N

W → e

ha

Titanic is sailing to Frand then queens town I reland.

FIGURE 13–2C

I suspect that there are other salutary benefits as well. I have observed that drawing seems to have a calming, centering effect on boys. They think while they draw, and this thinking pays dividends in the old-fashioned definition of writing (text). I'd like to see boys get the clear message that drawing is neither a punishable offense nor merely a way to decorate finished writing but a useful way to think through and flesh out the story, poem, or report they are writing.

Boys' sketches and drawings have a distinctive quality. Girls draw nouns, boys draw verbs, Leonard Sax explains in his book *Why Gender*

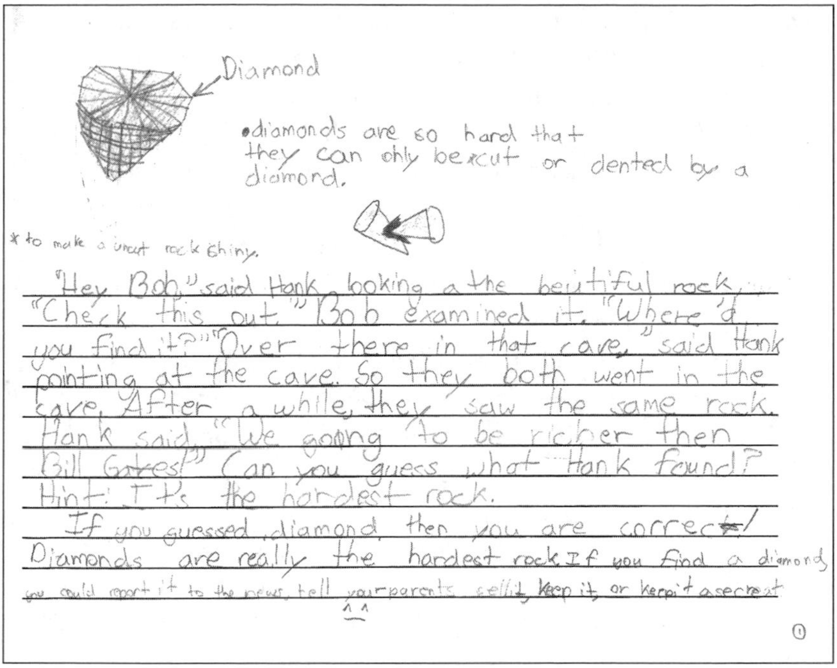

Diamond

• diamonds are so hard that they can only be cut or dented by a diamond.

* to make a uncut rock shiny.

"Hey Bob," said Hank, looking at the beautiful rock. "Check this out." Bob examined it. "Where'd you find it?" "Over there in that cave," said Hank pointing at the cave. So they both went in the cave. After a while, they saw the same rock. Hank said "We going to be richer then Bill Gates!" Can you guess what Hank found? Hint: It's the hardest rock.

If you guessed diamond, then you are correct! Diamonds are really the hardest rock. If you find a diamond you could report it to the news, tell your parents, sell it, keep it, or keep it a secret.

①

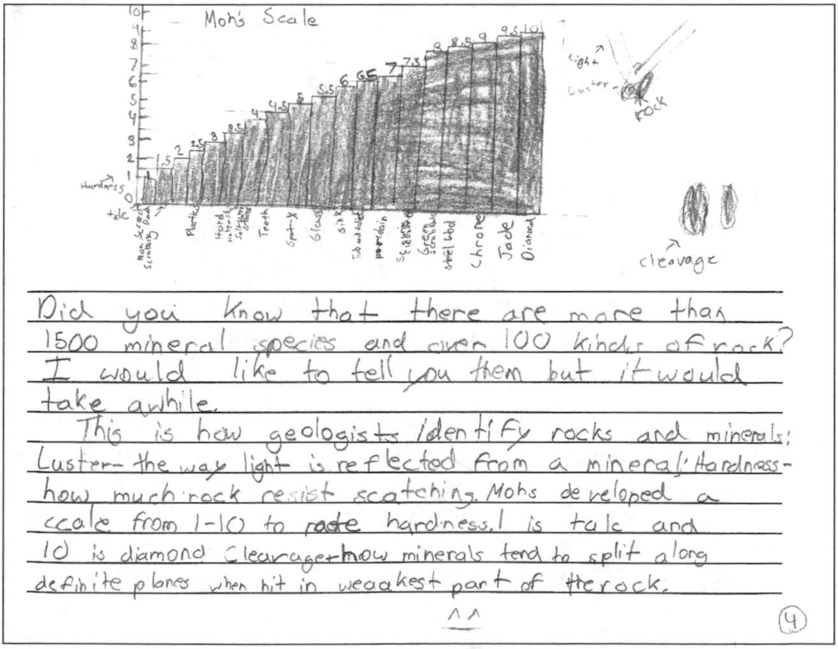

Did you know that there are more than 1500 mineral species and over 100 kinds of rock? I would like to tell you them but it would take awhile.

This is how geologists identify rocks and minerals: Luster— the way light is reflected from a mineral. Hardness— how much rock resist scatching. Mohs developed a scale from 1-10 to rate hardness. 1 is talc and 10 is diamond. Cleavage— how minerals tend to split along definite planes when hit in weakest part of the rock.

④

FIGURES 13–3A AND 13–3B PAGES FROM "ROCKS," BY PAULUS ABUAKEL.

Matters (2005, p. 23). Christopher Wadsworth, executive director of the International Boys' Schools Coalition, agrees. When left to their own devices, he says, girls tend to draw nouns (people and faces), whereas boys are drawn to verbs (action shots and bombs going off).

From my own observations of boys' and girls' drawings, this generalization rings true. Boys use their drawings to pump up the action in their narratives. I often say to young writers, "Nouns make the pictures, verbs make those pictures move." Drawings provide boys with another way of doing the work of verbs.

Boys who are skilled artists achieve a high status in the classroom. Teachers recognize their skill. Nevertheless we remain suspicious of drawing, and I'm not quite sure why. Perhaps we consider it time off-task or feel nervous that drawing is a distraction that pulls kids away from real writing.

But the whole concept of "real writing" is in flux. In Chapter 9, Linda Silverman argues that keyboarding, not handwriting, represents the future of writing. A similar argument could be made about drawing.

"The very definition of 'text' is changing," notes Tom Newkirk. "Go to any website and you'll find lots of new ways of communicating information: flash animation, streaming videos, cartoons, interactive chat, and so forth."

Encouraging students to draw allows them to participate in this brave new visual world—a world that is familiar to them. Alas, today we see recess, music, and art disappearing from many schools.

"In this political climate teachers are forced to consider: how does the use of drawing relate to preparing a child to succeed on a test?" points out Mike McCormick, a recently retired fifth-grade teacher in Eagle River, Alaska. "A teacher who looks at the development of writing as a journey lasting throughout a student's life is more likely to find the use of drawing a helpful aid in the development of a young writer (and more defensible to parents and administrators)."

What Can I Do in My Classroom?

As writing teachers, we cannot impose a one-size-fits-all writing process. Rather, we must help each student find a process that works for him or her. For boys this process should include drawing, which gives them another symbolic system they can use to communicate their ideas. Boys love to draw; allowing boys to draw while writing will make it more fun and help them feel invested. If nothing else you'll notice an immediate uptick in their engagement. I urge teachers to:

✖ Embrace a more visual definition of writing that includes sketches and drawing.

✖ Allow boys not merely to "sketch to stretch" but also to "sketch to compose."

✖ Show an interest in their drawings. Honor their drawings by giving them the same level of respect we give their written words: "Tell me about this part of the story. What's happening over here?"

✖ Encourage students to use their writer's notebooks as a sketch book. Invite them to include drawings as well as words.

✖ Create mini-lessons that model specific drawing techniques and strategies.

✖ Share models of books with boys as artists. (*Max's Logbook* by Marissa Moss is a good example.)

Moss-E-Field 2004–2005
Matt Valley, Grade 9

So where do we go from here? The first official year of the Moss-E-Field league is over. We were unable to finish due to snow. But overall it was an awesome year. I guess ORCSD un-officially won it all. This season has truly been the toughest of them all. We have lost a friend and role model Matthew Sarno. We have lost a community leader and friend's dad Steve Wilkinson. We have lost principals and superintendents. And we are now unfortunately on the edge of losing Greg's grandmother. A player's house has also burned down. It is hard to believe that this has all happened in a single year. It truly seems like a lot longer. It should have been. You're not supposed to lose that many people so close to you in such a short amount of time. But what some people do not understand. They do not get the fact the Moss-E-Field actually made us forget about our problems. We would play hours on end. If you have not played there you should and if you have had a chance you are truly lucky. You have experienced something so great. See every time I think of summer, the smell of grass or every time I pick up a tennis ball I think of Moss-E-Field. It has come from a game that kept us from dieing from being bored in the summer into a passionate league. It has made friendships. It has brought everybody closer together. It may sound a little cheesy but Moss-E-Field is a gift from god. This season was good but it was not the best. Coburn was the story of the year with his unbelievable stats. Nestea made an unbelievable playoff run, chomping down everyone in their way. Kegan Quimby put up big numbers. Valley finally found himself again. Gilmore got his arm back. I could continue for ever on all the good stuff that happened. But the reason it was not as good was because we were not as close. This summer did not feature as many sleepovers. Not many lake trips. Not much bonding off the field. So now we are left wondering. Who is retiring? Who is changing teams? Is the league expanding? Will Alden regain his batting title? And what ever happened to that kid named Matt Campbell? Time will tell us the answers. Winter is now here. Looking outside as I write this it is only four in the afternoon. It is starting to get dark and it seems impossible that over the summer some games were just starting. We could play till seven at night. Not worrying about homework or anything of that sort. Moss-E-Field is abandoned, waiting for hopefully another truly memorable summer. This upcoming season is inching closer to us with every given second. This could be our last season, so boys let's make this one count. Let's make this one better then the rest. Something we can remember our entire lives. Let's make it special.

Some background is helpful for this piece. It appeared on the whiffleball website by a boy who lives in my school district (http://www.mossefield.com). Recently we have suffered several tragic losses in the Oyster River School District (a beloved superintendent and principal, plus a high school boy). Matt touches on these losses in this sweet, end-of-childhood piece of boy writing. There's a great deal of depth here. It seems that sports, specifically his love of whiffleball, gives him a vehicle to channel his sense of loss.

Chapter 14

Help Wanted: Writing Genres That Appeal to Boys

If I were teaching, I would get boys out of the classroom. Take them to a swamp, dig through the muck, look for pollywogs. Then maybe take them back and have them look at pond water through slides and write up a lab report. They need hands-on activities. They get bored and distracted if you ask them to sit down and read a chapter and write up a paragraph—the kind of work that girls excel at.

Tom Mortenson

When JoAnn earned her doctorate from the University of New Hampshire we decided to throw a graduation party. Since JoAnn's heritage is part Lebanese, we thought Middle Eastern food might be appropriate for a summer party: hummus, pita bread, rolled grape leaves, tabouli, kibba, plus my personal favorite—small dough pockets containing spinach, onion, and mint. Some of my relatives drove up from Boston for the party, but I was chagrined to learn later that they *hated* the food we served. (They were too polite to say so at the time.) They left the party with empty stomachs, and had to grumpily search for a restaurant that served the kind of food they were accustomed to.

For many years writing workshops leaned heavily on one "food": the reliable, if sometimes boring, personal narrative. Recently we have expanded the menu in writing classrooms, and that's a good thing. But in many schools the writing menu mainly consists of genres that hold little interest for boys. Like my disgruntled relatives, these boys leave our classrooms feeling hungry and unsatisfied. They are forced to go find another place where they can get what they really want.

The Dominance of Personal Narrative

The writing process movement begat the writing workshop format, which, from its infancy, put the highest premium on realistic personal narratives and emotionally sincere poetry. For years we preached our message—*write what you know and write from the heart*—and I should know because I was there. For a long time personal narrative dominated the writing curriculum. This seemed like a fine idea at the time, and personal stories can be a natural way for kids to find their stride as writers. But perhaps we have been blind to the limitations of such an approach.

In an article published in *Language Arts*, Brenda Power (1995) critiqued writing process pedagogy as privileging the "confessional poet" kind of writing (one that values emotion and self-disclosure) above others. If this has been true—and I think it has—we have elevated a kind of writing that boys may not be interested in, or very good at. The overemphasis on realistic narrative and sincere expressive writing has put boy writers at a relative disadvantage to girl writers. (David Booth, Jeff Wilhelm, and other writers have pointed out a similar thing in school reading; whereas boys typically prefer to read fantasy and nonfiction, the reading curriculum usually gives kids a heavy dose of realistic fiction, literature that emphasizes introspection/reflection over plot/action.)

"I think that the girls enjoy writing about the inner conflicts and issues they face," says Holly Martocci, a sixth-grade language arts teacher in Connecticut. "Many girls consider writing for release and reflection on their feelings. In my observations, most sixth-grade boys are not as interested in accessing and understanding their *feelings* as girls are."

Susannah Voigt, an English teacher in Brooklyn, shared a similar insight. "I've been noticing this year that the boys I'm working with are really unhappy with the more reflective writing we ask them to do," she told me. "The first unit we did this year was memoir writing, and many of the boys HATED it. I really had to negotiate, modify, cajole—and I was thinking, maybe these writing units, produced at this largely female academic institution, are somehow gendered. Maybe fourteen-year-old boys don't want to do this kind of lyrical-reflective writing. The girls, on the other hand, were perfectly happy to do it, almost without exception."

Certainly there is value in showing kids that actual experiences from their own lives can be a great resource for any writer to draw upon. But a steady diet of personal narrative has turned off many boys who would prefer to compose wilder, edgier, more fantastic action pieces of writing, or write about characters borrowed from popular culture.

While working in writing classrooms I have had countless boys ask me, "Do we have to write about something real? Can't we make up stories?"

"No, I want you to write something true," I explained.

"Do we have to?" they persisted.

"Yes." And I could hear the air seeping out of the room.

"I understand the theory behind having kids write personal narrative first," says Kathleen Fay, reading teacher and coauthor of *Becoming One Community* (Fay and Whaley 2004). "But the fact is that there are those children who really want to write about Power Rangers. Sure, it may not lead to great writing, but those kids aren't engaged otherwise. They actually can write a narrative about Power Rangers."

As writing teachers we need to view the designated genres through the eyes of our boys. We need to ask: Given a choice, what genres do boys really like to write? Will any of the ones I'm planning for my class get the boys excited? There are many "boy-genre" possibilities, including some we may never have considered for the writing workshop.

"Cartoons are very popular with boys when choice is completely free," Max Brand says of his own students. "Cartoons are a wonderful genre for them to develop their own characters, explain their thinking in code to each other, and impress their buddies."

Other genres of interest to boys might include:

✘ Sports writing
✘ Sports commentary
✘ Creative nonfiction

* Fantasy
* Science fiction
* Movie or TV scripts
* Horror
* Graphic novels
* Comic books

Conventional wisdom says boys prefer to read and write nonfiction. I wondered if this is true and asked 242 boys, What's your favorite genre to write about? I gave them four choices: personal narrative, poetry, fiction, and nonfiction. The results can be seen in Figure 14–1.

This would suggest that if one of our fundamental goals is to engage boy writers we should make sure to include fiction in the curriculum, a genre many teachers avoid because it sprawls in so many different directions and can be difficult to teach.

"I don't often run across boys writing fantasy anymore," Carl Anderson says. "I think this is because the writing workshop has become too scripted. There are way too many genre studies. In some classrooms, kids rarely if ever get to choose which genres they write in. I believe this isn't good for boys *or* girls because limiting the genres that kids write in limits the purposes they can have as writers across the year, but I think this may hurt boys more since many of the genres that they enjoy writing in, such as comic books, fantasy, parody, etcetera, aren't included in the canon of genres that teachers typically include in their curriculum calendars."

When choosing a writing genre there are certain parameters or conditions to consider. First, we should be able to find evidence of such writing living in the world outside of school. Book reviews are a genre; book reports are not. When the writing exists in the real world—an op-ed piece in the newspaper, a feature article in a magazine, a graphic novel—students and teachers can venture forth in many different directions to study it. This might include finding out:

What are the historical roots of the genre? Where did it come from? Is anyone responsible for inventing it?
Where can examples of the genre be found?
Who are some well-known practitioners of this genre?
What are conventions of the genre?

Personal Narrative	Poetry	Fiction	Nonfiction
19	13	164	46

FIGURE 14–1

Whatever the genre, I suggest students don't start writing until they have been marinated in plenty of different models of the genre. We might invite kids to read pieces aloud, share them in pairs, make photocopies so they can underline or star favorite lines, copy certain passages into a writer's notebook, and so on. The purpose of this deep reading is to study the craft of the genre. Eventually students will want to try their hand at writing it. Eighth grader Alden Quimby wrote "A Season to Remember" (p. 107) after studying Rick Reilly columns that appeared on the back page of *Sports Illustrated*.

When students are working in a genre that is brand-new to the teacher (graphic novels, for example) there will be less teacher-to-student instruction and more side-by-side learning where the student and teacher work together to learn about it. Such a situation can make us feel scared or inadequate, but when it exists you've got genuine inquiry, a rare commodity in schools today.

Like the other chapters in this book, this one urges us to revise our teaching. But change is hard; it's very difficult to alter old habits. Case in point: a friend recently recommended *Dear Fish*, a picture book by Chris Gall. I bought the book sight unseen. It's a fanciful tale about a boy who writes a letter to fish. Suddenly fish start showing up all over his house, yard, street, and town. *Dear Fish* reminded me of *Tuesday* by David Wiesner, that surreal book where frogs start floating into the sky.

"Is this one good?" JoAnn asked when she saw *Dear Fish* on my nightstand.

"It's very imaginative," I said, showing her. "But it's not exactly what I expected. I don't know how I could use it in a writing workshop because it's completely unrealistic."

As soon as I spoke those words I heard them and stopped, appalled. I had met the enemy and it was me! I had so deeply assimilated the idea that students must write realistic ("true") stories, I was about to eliminate *Dear Fish*, a book full of whimsy and fantasy that boys would love, a book that might inspire boys and girls to produce some fanciful writing. I share this story to illustrate the unsettling truth that the most important obstacles we face may be the internal ones. If we are going to create "boy-friendlier" writing classrooms we must begin by taking an honest look inside ourselves.

What Can I Do in My Classroom?

A teacher friend of mine mentally divides the charts and posters that hang in her classroom into three categories: she constructs one-third of the print material herself, her students make another third, and the last third gets created together throughout the school year. This might be an apt model for constructing a menu of writing genres. If we truly believe that at least some of the curriculum should be negotiated between teachers and students, it follows that boys should have their needs and desires represented when it comes to what kind of writing they do.

✖ When creating your menu of genres or units of study, take into consideration the appetites of your boys. Give their interest and engagement as much weight as whether the genre "covers the curriculum."

✖ As you create your yearlong curriculum plan, or map for writing, try to include at least two genres that will be of high interest to them.

✖ Take a chance and let kids write in one genre you've never tried before.

✖ As with all genre studies, set a clear date for both the beginning and the ending. Make time for a celebration at the end so students have closure.

My Grandfather

Carter White, Grade 3

Blinded from the light
Above
Him my helpless grandfather
Lays
In his bed.

The light bright gray, calm, and
Blinding.

I walk in and see him.
I feel sad yet I
Feel happy that he is
Getting better.

He looks at
Me with
Dull eyes and a
Pale
Pale
Pale face
I hear footsteps outside the room
Sounds of
Runny noses and
People wiping away tears.
I leave the room.
I look back and
See the tube in his
Arm.
A sick face.

When I shut the door
I wonder
What does he feel
Like?
Will he have cancer

Again?
Was he sad like we
Were?

 I was really struck by the blinding light, an image that is repeated within the first seven lines. You can really sense the love Carter feels for his grandfather, but that word is never used. There's nothing fancy going on here. It just goes to show that kids don't need to use seventy-five-cent words or clever metaphors to create a memorable piece of poetry.

Chapter 15

Boy-Friendly Territory

In my writer's notebook, alongside some of my observational poetry, I wrote a handful of prayers. Sort of a new genre for me at the time (a couple years back when we were making a difficult move back to the States), but I mustered up enough courage to share one of them with the class when introducing the idea of taking risks in your writer's notebook. I think modeling my writing gave my boys a certain permission to write freely, and not to satisfy anyone but themselves. Their enthusiasm after that truly excited me!

Todd Frimoth, fifth-grade teacher

I'm standing inside Rye Airfield, in North Hampton, New Hampshire. It's a cavernous indoor skateboard park with all manner of interlocking ramps, half-pipes, grinding rails, and various-sized "bowls." The wire fences and concrete give the place an ugly look, at least to my eyes, although I know my thirteen-year-old son Joseph considers it beautiful.

On any given weekend day, this place attracts fifty to seventy-five teenagers, nearly all of them boys, eager to skateboard, Rollerblade, or practice tricks on their bikes. But today the park is not open for regular skating. Instead a large crowd of teenagers has gathered to watch Mike Valley, professional skateboarder, perform a special demonstration. Hundreds of boys have packed the perimeter, standing shoulder to shoulder, resting their skateboards upright as they watch. My son stands among them. With rapt attention the boys watch Valley soar through the air, making a 540 twist with a toe-grab. He successfully lands this jump, prompting the boys to roar their approval and bang their skateboards against the floor, a deafening combination that makes my ears hurt.

Watching all these boys, it occurs to me that a few hundred years ago the same scene would have taken place except they all would have been warriors, pounding their spears against the ground, sounding the war cry the moment before battle.

What conditions exist to create an environment where boys are truly engaged to learn? A skateboarding exhibition features lots of action, physical movement, and genuine drama (bravery in the face of danger). There is the presence of a powerful mentor. As Valley performs his tricks the boys watch closely, studying the master's technique, knowing that very soon they will be testing their skills in this arena.

This scene describes an arena in which boys are engaged in a learning situation outside of school. But is real engagement possible for boys *in* school? Where are the classrooms that engage boys? As it turns out they do exist, and it's worth thinking about what makes them successful.

At a summer lacrosse camp my son Robert (a high school sophomore) ran into John Silverio, who had been Robert's fifth-grade teacher. A sinewy guy in his forties, John Silverio has a coach's no-nonsense demeanor; kids treat him with affection and respect.

"We had a lot of fun that year," Robert said, smiling.

"Yeah, I still remember that class," John agreed.

I remember it, too, because it was a great year for Robert, the kind you'd want your kid to have every year. Robert loved fifth grade. Other adults I know, parents of boys and girls, have said the same thing. Robert's class did lots of reading and writing, but John built in an unusual number of activities. This word is sometimes used to describe classroom work done in small groups. In John Silverio's class these activities were wear-old-clothes-you're-going-to-get-dirty experiences that reflected his personal passions:

✖ Native American studies. This was a theme that ran through the entire year. Kids studied Native American peoples who lived in New Hampshire. One highlight was the evening when Robert and the other students went through an actual sweat-lodge purification ceremony, something Robert won't soon forget.

   In preparation for the ceremony students were asked to choose their own Native American name and to create a legend for how they got that name. At the sweat lodge there was a "naming ceremony," during which each student read aloud the name they had chosen for themselves. Robert, who has been a nonstop talker since he learned to speak, came up with the name Chattering Monkey. Even today we often call him by that name.

✖ Lacrosse. Silverio taught the kids how the game of lacrosse was invented by Native Americans. He has been the lacrosse coach at the University of New Hampshire, so it's no accident that dozens of fifth-grade boys that year signed up to play lacrosse in the spring. With their helmets, sticks, and padding, they looked to me like little warriors, eagerly heading off to battle. Five years later many of these boys are still playing lacrosse.

✖ The "Gridiron Challenge." This was a wildly popular unit during which kids used various math skills to track the scores and statistics of their favorite football teams.

✖ Salmon egg release. For this activity, students loosed salmon eggs into the local river.

✖ Model tree-house unit. John worked with tech ed teacher Al Lofgren. Each student designed and constructed a small wooden tree house, and then wrote a story about it.

I asked John to reflect on what he did to so successfully engage the boys in the learning that took place in his classroom. Did he think that being a man himself made it easier for him to relate to the boys in his class?

"I'm not sure that makes a difference," he replied. "Let's face it, there are a lot of very good female Language Arts teachers in the district that do an amazing job getting both genders to write."

I suggested that John created the kind of classroom where boys in particular would be excited to learn, but he seemed reluctant to embrace this idea.

"I feel I've been able to develop writing opportunities that are of interest to both males and females," he said. "I have girls that didn't know a thing about football who write these amazing end-of-the-season sports articles about their gridiron teams. On the other hand, I have been able to get boys to write fantasy stories in the past. I work hard at making connections with kids, and they realize that they are expected to perform at their best."

A Boys Writing Club

After I heard that Jennifer Allen had started a Boys Writing Club at her school in Waterville, Maine, I was sufficiently intrigued to drive three hours north so I could check it out.

Jennifer Allen had started the club with a group of fifth-grade boys. When I arrived she met me and took me to her classroom. A few minutes later members of the Boys Writing Club began appearing in Jen's room, one by one. I counted nine boys. They sat at a long table, took out their lunches, and began to eat. The boys quickly included me in the group; we had a spirited conversation during lunch.

Soon the boys took out their notebooks and stories. The most confident ones began to read. Some encouraged other boys to read. I noticed a few boys quietly slide a notebook over to Jennifer so she could push it forward for me to read or read it aloud herself.

Devin began by reading a story about the day his dog died. His story included a very poignant part where his father allowed the kids to go into the house, two by two, to have one last special time with the dog before it got put to sleep.

"That was sad, but good," Jamie told Devin.

"Thanks." Devin looked over at Mark. "Read 'Blub!'"

"But you've already heard it," Mark protested.

"But he hasn't!" Sam said, nodding at me.

"Okay," Mark sighed, obviously pleased to be asked. He read aloud his piece about getting a Siamese fighting fish as a pet. (See "Bettaie" p. 17) When Mark finished, the boys murmured appreciatively.

"Read the one about the hockey fights" (see p. 53), Mark suggested to Thomas. One by one they read aloud their stories. Jen Allen made a few comments, but definitely did not run the club. The boys looked at each other at least as much as they looked at her. I was struck by the feeling of support and encouragement in that room. There was no critique, no you-should-do-this, not one discouraging word. Those boys were really there for each other.

My visit came at a fortunate time because that was the day Jen had chosen to launch a fourth-grade writing club. That afternoon she planned to have a preliminary meeting with some interested fourth-grade boys. Jen suggested that the fifth graders come and explain to the fourth-grade boys what the Boys Writing Club was all about. First, half a dozen fourth graders arrived, shyly sitting at the long table. At 2 p.m. the older boys arrived—Thomas, Devin, Sam, James, Jamie. Jennifer addressed them first.

"Maybe you could tell the fourth graders what the writing club is about," she suggested.

"It's great," Sam blurted out. "You can write whatever you want."

"Yeah, no prompts," Jamie said. "Never!"

"If you want to write fiction, you can write fiction," Thomas explained. "If you want to write poems, write poems. Nobody's telling you what to write."

"Yeah, and if you don't want to read anything you don't have to," Devin said.

The fourth graders just listened. They looked interested, if slightly bewildered by the enthusiastic descriptions coming from the older boys.

"Hey, look." Thomas pointed to the floor behind me. "Ants!"

Glancing down I saw a trail of ants on the linoleum.

"Lemme see!" Three of the fifth-grade boys jostled one another and got onto their hands and knees. Forgetting their charge to explain the Boys Writing Club, the fifth graders began pressing their thumbs to the floor, systematically killing the ants.

I asked Jen to describe the genesis of the Boys Writing Club.

"I had just finished a writing workshop in a fourth-grade class-room when the classroom teacher asked me if I had a minute to look at some boys' writing," Jen explained. "She nodded to one of the boys, and soon I found myself surrounded by five boys, all waving their writing in front of me. They had pages and pages of writing. I was a bit stunned, since these were the same boys who were typically resistant writers within the classroom and moaned that they had nothing to write about just minutes ago when I was visiting during their writer's workshop.

"They begged to read their stories to me. I stood in the hallway surrounded by eager writers waving pages of crumbled, smeared papers. These boys took turns reading aloud their stories. Their stories contained dragons, characters with superpowers, and lots of action—all writing that had been generated at home on their own time.

"They asked if they could write with me during a recess. These kids were asking me to write with them, the very students I had been struggling to reach in the classroom. Four of the five boys were targeted to receive supplemental support as struggling readers. How could I turn them down? That's how it started."

In recent years there has been a renewed interest in single-sex schools. I asked Jen, "What made you narrow the writing club to boys?"

"That just happened by chance," she replied. "The boys approached me. If it had been a group of girls or a mixed-gender group that had approached me, I would have offered them the same invitation."

After school that day I interviewed several members of the Boys Writing Club, including a fifth grader named Sam Zarfos.

RALPH: What do you like about the Boys Writing Club?

SAM: I like being able to write your own stories, let it flow out the way you want it to. If you're happy you can give a little slow part, but then suddenly shock them. And you have your friends that you can write with and get ideas off of. In class you can't talk to them— you have to think on your own.

RALPH: It seems like the kids in the Boys Writing Club are very supportive of each other.

SAM: (nodding) Yes.

RALPH: It could be competitive: who's the best, who's the second best, but you guys all seem generous to each other.

SAM: Sometimes it is competitive. And people can know who's actually better than them, or who they've caught up to. I mean, I know I'm not the best in that group in writing. Maybe someday I could be.

RALPH: What do you think about writing workshop in your regular class? What's wrong with it? How could you make it better?

SAM: Well, maybe take a vote on what kind of writing we want to do: nonfiction, fiction, realistic fiction . . . And maybe we could have more time. The way it is now, we've got one day, pretty much, to come up with a rough draft, and for your final draft you've got three or four.

RALPH: So you'd like more time?

SAM: More time, and freedom to choose what we want to write about. I try to think of you, how you have your own freedom and what you want to write about. I mean, that would be perfect!

RALPH: Are you a writer?

SAM: In part of fourth grade I thought I would never be able to do writing, ever. In first, second, and third I thought of myself as an awesome writer. If I wanted to I thought I could become an author, not as great as those people out there today, but maybe just one of those authors that are fun to read here and there.

RALPH: What happened in fourth grade? How did you lose your confidence?

SAM: People started putting me down . . . I lost my confidence and got two Cs on my writing. It just made me feel, "Well, maybe I can't do this, after all." And since I told myself that, it sort of turned out that way.

RALPH: Had you joined the Writing Club last year?

SAM: No, I had not joined it last year.

RALPH: So it sounds like last year wasn't such a great year for you.

SAM: No, it was not. This year is going better. This year the only reason I joined the group was one of my friends was talking about it, and he asked me if I wanted to join it. And I thought about it and I thought: here's my chance to write freely.

RALPH: You have to give up your recess, right?

SAM: (*quickly*) I don't care.

RALPH: You don't?

SAM: No, I don't care! I mean, we've got sports we can do at home when we've done our homework. We can play in the snow.

RALPH: You'd rather be writing in here than playing outside?

SAM: Yes. See, it's Friday. Friday is the day when the kids are even more bossy, and even more bullying to you. I say that 25 percent of my reason for coming here is, no, not even that, 10 maybe, or 15, is coming here to get away from those bullies. But the rest is because I really want to write my free stories.

RALPH: Have you ever had the experience of wanting to write about something but the teacher steered you away from it?

SAM: Yes. In third I wanted to work on one of my fictional stories. But at that time MEAs were coming out.

RALPH: What are MEAs?

SAM: Maine Educational Assessment.

RALPH: So you had to get ready for the test.

SAM: (*sadly*) Yeah, I had to get ready for the test.

RALPH: I see. Tell me, what's the hardest part of writing for you?

SAM: Like I told you, keeping that grip on the reader as you come into the full start of the story. But if I get past that, and I still have them [readers], then I'm just going to get them more. Because my middle, that's my hot spot.

RALPH: Do you share your writing with your family? Parents?

SAM: (*softly*) Sometimes.

RALPH: Are they interested?

SAM: Yeah.

RALPH: Do they give you the kind of feedback you want?

SAM: Yeah, if you mean do they say—"You're doing great, keep it going." That's exactly what I get from them, no more, no less. If you try and ask your parents for a suggestion on your writing then they could get the wrong idea for your story, and they could lead you the wrong way from where you wanted to go on your story.

RALPH: But in a writing conference isn't the teacher trying to give you ideas for your story, too?

SAM: They want us to come up with our own ideas.

RALPH: How do you see the teacher's role in the writing conference?

SAM: I think they're trying to help you make your story more but without leading you the wrong way, if you're already on the right way.

RALPH: Are those conferences helpful?

SAM: Sometimes. Sometimes it just gets to be a little bit more confused so I just keep going with the way I was pretty sure at the beginning I should go, and it usually turns out fine.

RALPH: One last thing. How would you complete this sentence: When we write in school, I wish we were allowed to . . . ?

SAM: (*without hesitation*) Write freely.

Sam's responses shed light not only on his writing concerns (tests, revisions) but also on other important issues (i.e., bullying) that affect boys. This interview got me thinking about the Boys Writing Club.

When I spoke to Jennifer Allen later I came back to the question of gender and asked if she thought there were advantages to its being limited to boys.

"I think there are advantages in the single-sex setting in learning how boys learn best," she told me. "These boys' learning styles hit me in the face—talking over one another, the need for movement, how they integrate illustrations and comics into their stories. I'm not sure we allow enough of their interests to surface in the classroom. I think by having them together they feel heard, listened to, respected. I work hard not to tell them to lower their voice, sit, etcetera . . . even though I secretly want to!"

What Can I Do in My Classroom?

A skateboard exhibition, a fifth-grade classroom, and a Boys Writing Club—what do they have in common? What can we learn from them in terms of creating an environment where boys are engaged to learn? Although these three environments are unique, they each possess common characteristics that should be part of every classroom:

✖ A strong social component—the boys work together, side by side, with lots of "cross-talk."
✖ An active environment—an emphasis on doing rather than talking about it.
✖ An abiding sense of fun and play.
✖ Choice. Even in John Silverio's class, where most of the high-interest activities are initiated by the teacher, students had a great deal of choice in determining what they wanted to build/create/write.
✖ The presence of a strong mentor. This person both sets an example and establishes a structure with clear guidelines. As we see from Jennifer Allen, *this mentor does not have to be male*. I can't emphasize this point enough. I have seen many female teachers who do a remarkable job of reaching out to their boys, listening to them, finding common ground, and helping them become more confident writers.

Chapter 16

Dramatic Transformations

Most kids, especially boys, have to write a lot of crap in order to produce something worthwhile. Many teachers want and expect a well-crafted three- or five-paragraph first draft. This is not going to happen with boys.

Arthur Voigt, literacy consultant

W e want boys to grow up with a self-image that says: *I'm a soccer player. I am a reader. I am a citizen. I am a writer.* Conventional wisdom would dictate that having a confident self-image as a writer cannot happen overnight but must grow gradually over time.

Here's a surprise—it *can* happen overnight. It turns out that even a boy who feels as if he has lost every writing battle can win this war with one meaningful experience. In responding to my boy questionnaire, many kids who checked "Yes" to "I am a writer" attributed it to one year, one teacher, one powerful writing experience. Here are three brief examples.

1. "I trace my son's view of himself as a writer to middle school when he had a couple of quite mean-spirited teachers," a friend of mine told me. "These people were well known for this to other teachers and the administration, who seemed powerless to do anything

151

about it. My son was nominated by his peers to give the graduation speech for his class. He saw this as an opportunity for
revenge.

"His first drafts took a slash-and-burn approach, naming
names and pulling no punches. I tried to persuade him that it's best
not to put other people on the defensive by offending, that a thousand paper cuts were better than a hatchet job (I could not get him
to give up the idea of some degree of revenge), and that the best
revenge is to do something that everyone else admires. He worked
hard at it and took very little feedback after that, but he under-
stood the point.

"The final talk was very funny and in one little place he subtly
nailed those two teachers to the wall. He got a standing ovation
and, for three or four years after, kids and even the odd parent
asked if they could get a copy. I think that experience transformed
him into someone who saw himself as a writer. He saw what he
could do with writing."

2. Fourth grade was the year my son Joseph started seeing himself as
a writer. His teacher that year was Steven Tullar. Steve was assisted
by Pete Schiat, a former fifth-grade teacher who came out of
retirement to work with the class on a regular basis. Schiat taught
the kids a form of prose poetry known as "Nature's Eye." Those
students wrote every day, and they became adept at describing
what they saw in nature. This genre encouraged students to carefully observe the world, something many boys excel at. Here's a
sample that Joseph wrote that year.

*The cat sits on the dusty wood ledge waiting and waiting and watch-
ing the pinkish sky above which stretched acros the universe. Then
she slowly looks at the yellow orange and red woods. The trees tow-
ering over her makes her look very, very, very, very tiny, but she
doesn't seem to notice. She jumps off the oak ledge and heads toward
the tangle of trees leaves and branches. Her tail flicks up as she
walks. She looks around and stops to sniff at an acorn, then scampers
into the woods and vanishes out of sight.* (See Figure 16–1.)

Joseph produced dozens of Nature's Eye pieces like this. He
was guided and inspired by two powerful mentors who signaled
that it's okay to write about nature. He had the opportunity to

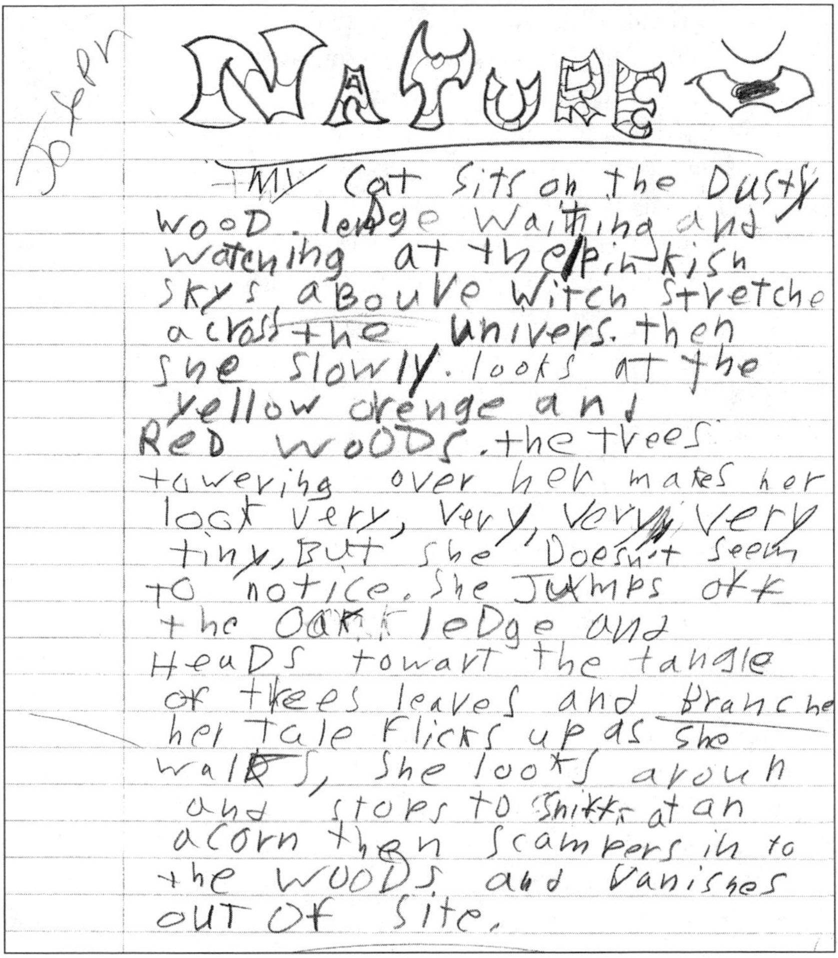

FIGURE 16–1 JOSEPH'S NATURE'S EYE PIECE.

write a Nature's Eye piece just about every day. In addition his teachers were thoughtful about audience. The boys were encouraged to write for themselves, to enjoy their own work, but Tullar and Schiat also scheduled periodic celebrations where kids got the chance to read aloud their Nature's Eye pieces to other students, parents, and grandparents. During that year I saw a remarkable thing—Joseph, along with many other boys and girls, turning into writers right before my eyes.

3. Jolene DiBrango, a fifth-grade teacher, worked with one very resistant writer named Justin. "His former teachers told me that he hated to write and they were correct," Jolene said. "Justin pro-

fessed his hatred on the very first day of class. It wasn't until our
poetry unit that things clicked for him for the very first time. He
was an avid and very talented soccer player. He was attentionally
challenged for sure and all he wanted to write about was soccer.
He would start drafts of narratives but they never quite worked.
Then one day I showed the class a poem on basketball written by
a professional poet. The poem had short lines describing the feel
of basketball, the sounds of basketball, and what it felt like to score
a basket."

"Foul Shot"
Edwin A. Hoey

With two 60's stuck on the scoreboard
And two seconds hanging on the clock,
The solemn boy in the center of eyes,
Squeezed by silence
Seeks out the line with his feet,
Soothes his hands along his uniform,
Gently drums the ball against the floor,
Then measures the waiting net,
Raises the ball on his right hand,
Balances it with his left,
Calms it with fingertips,
Breathes,
Crouches,
Waits, and then through a stretching of stillness,
Nudges it upward.

The ball
Slides up and out,
Lands,
Leans,
Wobbles,
Wavers,
Hesitates,
Exasperates,
Plays it coy
Until every face begs with unsounding screams—

And then
And then
And then,

Right before ROAR-UP
Dives down and through. *(Hoey 1994)*

"Justin sat down and wrote one just like that about soccer," Jolene says. "Sharon Creech's book *Love That Dog* taught him that it was okay to borrow a poet's style. The next day we conferenced, and I was blown away by Justin's poem."

"Soccer"

I dribble, dribble
Pass
Then
score.
containing, angling
fake out, breakaway, goal
penalties, free kicks
my salty sweat
passing to myself
against the wall
tripped
over
over
again
ref not calling
I say
"ref watch that kid"
diving
scraped knee
"goal kick"
ref calls
sacrifice to hit the ball
boom
bang
off my foot it goes
chip shot goal!!!

Buzzer . . . aaahh
second half
watching the goalie's eye
run
get it
shoot
corner net
GOAL!!!

"I couldn't contain my excitement," Jolene told me. "I took his hand and squeezed it tightly as I discussed all he had done well. I made a copy of his poem, placed it on the overhead, and we compared it to the basketball poem. The class thought that it was written by the same person, until I revealed Justin's name. He was grinning from ear to ear and so was I. On that day Justin became a writer, something he never thought he could be."

Justin later entered several poetry contests, was a finalist in one, and got published in two others. I asked Jolene what the crucial ingredients to Justin's transformation were. She credited writer's workshop, the book *Love That Dog*, and "Foul Shot" by Edwin A. Hoey. Jolene omitted the most important factor: herself. She encountered a boy everyone agreed was a poor writer, but Jolene didn't write him off. She never gave up on him. She has a right to take pride in his accomplishment.

I shared with a friend of mine the idea that some boys can become a writer in one dramatic transformation.

"That's interesting," she said. "But are you sure it's only true for boy writers? Couldn't that be true of girls, too?"

Honestly, I don't know the answer to this question. I make no claim that such sudden transformations are unique to boy writers. Even if they are not, I think this idea should bring solace to all of us who work with boys, even with those kids who have suffered through haphazard teaching and are burdened with a poor self-image.

Here's the good news: it's never too late. Despite everything that they've gone through, these boys can perk up and blossom if we give them a fresh start. We can make a difference. We can be the ones who help them turn the corner and start seeing themselves as writers.

Chapter 17

Boys and Writing: Persnickety Questions

Q: *What do you do when a kid "crosses the line" in his writing and goes too far?*

A: Let me say right off the bat that I'm wary of that phrase. Did Gary Paulsen cross the line when Harris pees on the electric fence in *Harris and Me* and he gets a shock in his genitals? Did Alden Quimby cross the line in "A Season to Remember" (p. 107) when he included the line, "I'd be blowin' my nose in Benjamin's and wipin' my butt with Grant's if I was rakin' in that kind of dough"? That certainly makes the point in a way that's hard to forget.

Q: *Many teachers would say that in that sentence he does cross the line. Surely not everything a boy writes is acceptable or appropriate. Aren't there limits?*

A: Sure. But the limits are subjective. Whether or not a writer crosses the line depends on the school and the teacher. Every situation is different. I'd avoid blanket rules about what is and isn't deemed appropriate in kids' writing. The boy's purpose is important as well. For instance, we should be more lenient with what goes into a kid's writer's notebook (private realm) than in the final project (public realm).

Q: *Okay, but still, what should a teacher do in a situation where he or she has to tell a kid to stop writing something?*

A: Do it. I would do it firmly but quietly. I think Max Brand's point is worth considering—with boys, saving face is important. I would avoid making this into a confrontation the whole class can see. Remember what the witch says in *The Wizard of Oz*, "These things must be done delicately."

Q: *How much violence should a teacher allow in boys' writing?*
A: This is a question that every teacher must answer for him or herself. Personally I don't see any reason why all the student samples in this book couldn't be shared and celebrated in a writing workshop. However, I recognize that the answer to this question depends on personal tastes, district rules, and the values of the community.

It would be interesting to have kids study a short story like "The Tell-Tale Heart" by Edgar Allan Poe. This famous story contains a murder, of course. But it's the psychological tension, not the graphic details, that give it such power.

Q: *How about a kid who uses humor in his writing to make fun of someone in the class or school?*
A: I'd certainly discourage that. It works against the community we need to create, and community is essential. But let me just say that the premise of your last few questions makes me uncomfortable. Why can't we be interested in rather than suspicious of boy writers? I think we're too conditioned to look at boys' behavior in the writing classroom, and what they do in their writing, as a problem that must be contained or managed lest the inmates run the prison (or however that saying goes). That kind of negative thinking reinforces itself. With all their quirks and passions, boy writers provide us with real opportunity. There's a great deal of energy if only we could harness it. Let's try to tap into their unique strengths.

Q: *You suggest teachers make room for more boy-friendly genres. Are you talking about revamping the writing curriculum?*
A: I'd describe it as a rebalancing. I think we have swung too far toward predetermined units of study. Yes, I realize there will still be kinds of writing we must teach, but let's include at least some genres that boys find stimulating.

Q: *Some boys find writing such a laborious process that they get turned off. What can we do for them?*

A: Ask ourselves, what can *this* boy realistically do in *this* piece of writing? Let him do that. If he wants to publish the piece then we might have to edit and retype the final draft.

Q: *Most kids hate to revise. Any suggestions?*

A: Don't force them to revise everything they write! William Stafford once said, "When I write something that interests me, I go back. If it doesn't interest me, I go on." Let's let boys "go on" and write something new instead of always having to rework what they just wrote. Whether to revise a particular piece, like what to write about, is a choice we must allow boys to make. On the other hand I think we should make it clear that we expect them to find some pieces they want to revise.

One other thing. When I think back on the times when my own boys were willing to revise, they usually involved projects the boys were engaged in where there was a clear purpose or outcome.

Q: *What about scripting or copying a kid's story?*

A: I think it's a great idea because it cuts through the tedious physical word that derails so many boys when they write. In *Even Hockey Players Read*, David Booth says, "We can record a boy's dictated story on the chalkboard or on chart paper, acting as a scribe, and then provide the boy with a copy of the story for rereading, so he will see his ideas and words in print" (2000, p. 67). Of course, copying a kid's writing takes time so it helps to get a volunteer (parent) to help with this.

Q: *You argue that boys should be allowed more drawing as part of their composing process. But isn't there a danger that drawing will take away precious time when they could be writing? Isn't drawing a way some boys avoid writing?*

A: We've got to stop thinking of writing and drawing as two separate things. They are two different symbolic systems. Let's try to conceive of drawing as part of the writing process itself.

Q: *Could drawings or illustrations be used to teach the writer's craft?*

A: Certainly. In our video series *When Students Write* (Fletcher and Portalupi 2002), Suzanne Whaley does a mini-lesson using a snowball rolling down a hill to teach kids about recurring lines in a text. The visual of the snowball and hill makes it so clear and tangible.

Take a look at the illustrations in David Shannon's *No, David!* On one page we see David with his mother, but we see only the mother's body, not her head. An illustration like that is a great way to teach kids about point of view. What kids learn from a drawing they can transfer to their writing, and vice versa.

Q: *This all sounds nice in theory. But if we create the kind of boy-friendly writing classrooms you describe, won't it disadvantage boys when they go to more traditional classes (i.e., high school English)?*

A: Consider three points: (1) There's no downside to getting kids engaged. That's *always* a plus; (2) if a boy connects to writing and feels confident as a writer he will bring that positive attitude and knowledge to other writing environments; (3) traditional English classes really aren't so traditional anymore. Many high schools and even more English classes ask students to write multigenre research papers. This summer the University of New Hampshire is offering a course in digital storytelling! Slowly, the canon is changing.

Q: *What do you think about writing as punishment?*

A: I'm totally against it. It creates a negative association (writing equals pain) in a boy's mind that lasts a long time. It works against everything I believe about nurturing strong, confident writers of either sex. Boys get writing-as-punishment far more often in school than girls do, by the way.

Q: *Let's talk about technology. In many cases kids have more "bells and whistles" when they write at home than in school. Does that create a problem for teachers?*

A: Yes, teachers can't always match that. Writing material does matter. David Booth says, "We can ensure that boys have access to a range of writing materials and tools, including special notepads, clipboards, graph paper, poster board, stationery, pens, markers, pencils, and, especially, computers" (2000, p. 67).

I've been thinking a lot about writing at home. It's interesting that when I gathered my son Robert's strongest pieces, I noticed that three-fourths of what I considered his best pieces had been written at home. At first I thought that this fact spoke poorly about his schooling. But Robert had wonderful writing teachers in elementary school. I think it's actually a credit to those teachers that he did so much writing at home. In fact, I think one could assess how effective a school literacy program is by how much writing and reading kids do at home.

Q: *In terms of writing at home, what might teachers look for?*

A: I simply think we should ask, What conditions are present (topics, time, response, privacy, visual literacy) that allow boys to write at home? The answers may be surprising.

Q: *Some teachers report that their girls are more engaged in keeping a writer's notebook than their boys. Do you have any suggestions for getting boys interested in the writer's notebook?*

A: In our society the idea of having a journal to record one's innermost thoughts and feelings is something sanctioned for girls. Anne Frank kept a diary. There have been various movies where girls write in their journals. Boys may not be as eager to delve into their emotions. But boys are collectors. (Of course many girls love to collect things, too.) I tell kids that I use my writer's notebook to collect fascinating quotes, weird facts, feathers, leaves, cards, cartoons, and so on. That idea—of the notebook as a place to collect interesting stuff (including lots of artifacts)—seems to resonate with boys.

Chapter 18

A Personal Note

> *If you treat boys like they're going to be a problem, acting up, writing silly, crude stuff, just trying to crack up the class, well, that's exactly how they'll be. They will rise to the level of your expectation. But if you embrace their world, treat them with respect, and take them seriously, the boys will write some meaningful things.*
>
> Cyrene Wells, literacy consultant

I was forty years old when Joseph was born. People say he looks like me, especially when we grin.

Age 2
He stands in the driveway wearing his baseball uniform, holding the bat, little belly sticking out, waiting for me to pitch to him. He insists that I sing "Take Me Out to the Ballgame," and I must sing it continuously while we play baseball. He hits the ball about once every four times. When he does hit one, he drops the bat and tears madly around the bases.

Age 3
I'm buckling Joseph into his stroller.

"When you're my age I'll be eighty-three years old," I tell him. "Imagine that? I'll be an old man. You *might have to push* me *in a wheelchair!*"

"I will," he solemnly promises. "I'll push you good, Daddy, and I won't never tip you over."

Age 7

I'm driving with Joseph past the University of New Hampshire, which is located two miles from our house.

"When I go to college I think I'm going to go to UNH," Joseph says. "That way when I have a free period, I can just walk down the street to our house."

"Maybe," I tell him. "It's hard to believe right now, but when you're old enough to go to college you might be ready to go to a different school in a whole new place."

"Oh, no, Daddy." He shakes his head. "I would never leave you."

Age 9

Joseph and I are in Dover, New Hampshire, waiting for Robert to finish his guitar lesson. We've got some time to kill so we stroll over toward Dunkin' Donuts. On the way we step over a railroad track.

"When I was about your age," I tell Joseph, "there was a railroad not too far from my house. My friends and I used to put *pennies on the rail. When the train came by it would squish the pennies."*

"Really?" he asks, amazed. "You did that on purpose?"

I nod. "We had to be really careful we weren't near the tracks when the train came by."

Joseph asks: "Did you ever put rocks on the track?"

"No, we didn't want to derail the train! Just pennies. After the train went by we'd run down to the track and find those smushed coins."

"Wow, Dad." He looks at me, eyes shining with admiration. "It sounds like you were a pretty cool kid!"

Age 12

I taught Joseph to ski, but by now he has far surpassed me. Streaking down the steepest trails, Joseph is fluid and fearless. One of his friends says his family might go to Colorado to ski next winter, and maybe Joseph could come along. Joseph badly wants to go.

"Can I, Dad?"

"That might be fun," I say. "I'd like to go, too."

He frowns at me. "You're not coming!"

Staring at him, I realize he's dead serious.

"Why not?" I ask. "Are you embarrassed at the way I ski? I'm a pretty good skier."

"No, you're not! You suck at skiing, Dad!"

"I'm not as good as you," I admit, "but I'm getting stronger."

"You're not getting better! You still ski with your skis way too far apart! You're not coming to Colorado!"

Excerpt from My Writer's Notebook

At 3:00 p.m. I am standing in the lobby of Moharimet Elementary School with a few dozen other parents, all of us waiting for our kids to be dismissed. It is one of those ugly December days, cold and rainy, and nobody is talking, or even smiling. Dennis Harrington, the principal, comes over the loudspeaker to announce that the "walkers" will be dismissed in one minute. Still, none of the parents speak. We are just a bunch of dark lights in the hallways. Then the bell rings and as children begin to appear the parents stand up, and one by one our faces get switched on. Then I see my son Joseph, and my face gets switched on, too.

I wrote this about Joseph but I could have shared similar snippets about my other boys—Robert, Adam, or Taylor. No doubt you have your own collection of memories involving sons, brothers, nephews, male students—all trying to cross the great river and make the difficult transition from infancy to manhood. Parents and teachers work hard to give boys the tools (skills, work ethic, experience, confidence, etc.) so one day they can prosper in the world at large.

How do we better nurture and support our struggling boy writers? In this book we've explored many different facets of this question. Although there are no magical answers, I'll leave you with four ideas.

✖ *Just let them write.* These four words nearly became the title for this book. Boy writers need time and real choice in order to get comfortable and find their stride. Before we push or prod them to write this or that genre, using this topic sentence or that concluding paragraph, I say let's get out of the way and make space for boys to write about their own subjects, including their own characters, plots, drawings, and jokes. This means creating classrooms that are less about us and more about them.

✖ *Take the long view.* Drinking a soda before a soccer game might give a kid extra energy for that game, but in the long run soda drinking is a bad way to become a strong, healthy athlete. In a similar way, test preparation might bump kids' scores in the short term but in the long run it works against the goal of helping kids make lasting connections to writing. Every assignment or activity in our classrooms should be put against the standard: will this serve my goal of creating lifelong writers?

✖ *Consider pleasure.* Most boys know how to read, but do they choose to read? If they experience pleasure while reading in school they will choose to read when they're away from school.

The same thing is true for writing. Most boys know how to write. And most will write in school, however reluctantly, if we give them specific assignments and tell them exactly what we want them to do. But do they choose to write when they're not in school?

It's not only girls who wanna have fun—boys do, too. Boys will invest the necessary time and energy, the sheer work inherent in writing, if they can feel some enjoyment while doing so. Let's make sure that boys are having fun in our writing classes.

✖ *Think relationships.* We're not teaching writing—we're teaching writers. For better and for worse, the kid who reads the grade on his paper or hears your spoken comments will take them to heart.

Writing is personal. We want every boy to connect with writing in a personal way, to say to himself: *Yeah, I can do that. I'm a writer.*

Teaching is personal, too. Nurturing boy writers begins by forging strong relationships. I've known administrators who think that being able to connect to kids is a knack that some teachers have and some don't. I disagree. I believe every one of us can connect with our boy students.

Think of a boy in your class: a Jarod, Xander, Max, Enrique, or Brad. He may seem cold, aloof, indifferent. It might look like he doesn't give a hoot whether or not you're interested in his life. But he does. Every day he watches, trying to decide if you like him or not. Even if you don't love this kid it's important to reach out to him so he can see that he's on your radar. Mention the sports team or rock group on his T-shirt. Inquire in a friendly way about what he does after school. Is he a collector? What does he write (or read) at home just for fun?

Encourage him to use words and phrases that sound like him. Allow him to do the writing only he can do. Let him see you react to and enjoy his writing. Create a classroom where he can reclaim his voice: the unique qualities of a writer's personality that show up on the page. That's the greatest gift he will take from you, and it will fuel him long after he leaves your class and goes on to write the future of his life.

Percentage of Students, by Writing Achievement Level and Gender, Grades 4, 8, and 12: 1998 and 2002

		Below Basic	At Basic	At Proficient	At Advanced	At or above Basic	At or above Proficient
Grade 4							
Male	1998	21 *	63	16 *	1 *	79 *	16 *
	2002	19	61	19	1	81	20
Female	1998	11 *	59 *	28 *	2 *	89 *	30 *
	2002	9	55	33	3	91	36
Grade 8							
Male	1998	22	61 *	17 *	# *	78	17 *
	2002	21	58	20	1	79	21
Female	1998	9	55 *	34 *	2 *	91	36 *
	2002	9	50	38	3	91	42
Grade 12							
Male	1998	30 *	56 *	14	#	70 *	14
	2002	37	49	13	1	63	14
Female	1998	14	58 *	27	1 *	86	29 *
	2002	15	52	30	3	85	33

\# Percentage rounds to zero.

* Significantly different from 2002.

Note: Percentages within each writing achievement level range may not add to 100, or to the exact percentages at or above achievement levels, due to rounding.

Source: U.S. Department of Education, Institute of Education Sciences, National Center for Education Statistics, National Assessment of Educational Progress (NAEP), 1998 and 2002 Writing Assessments.

Appendix B

For Every 100 Girls

Tom Mortenson
Postsecondary Education Opportunity
April 26, 2006

K–12 Education

For every 100 girls enrolled in gifted and talented programs in public elementary and secondary schools there are 94 boys enrolled. http://nces.ed.gov/programs/digest/d04/tables/dt04_055.asp.

For every 100 girls who graduate from high school 96 boys graduate. (NCES, unpublished tabulation).

For every 100 girls suspended from public elementary and secondary schools 250 boys are suspended. http://nces.ed.gov/programs/digest/d04/tables/dt04_144.asp.

For every 100 girls expelled from public elementary and secondary schools 335 boys are expelled. http://nces.ed.gov/programs/digest/d04/tables/dt04_144.asp.

Special Education

For every 100 girls diagnosed with a special education disability 217 boys are diagnosed with a special education disability. http://www.iteachilearn.com/uh/meisgeier/statsgov20gender.htm.

For every 100 girls diagnosed with a learning disability 276 boys are diagnosed with a learning disability. http://www.iteachilearn.com/uh/meisgeier/statsgov20gender.htm.

For every 100 girls diagnosed with emotional disturbance 324 boys are diagnosed with emotional disturbance. http://www.iteachilearn.com/uh/meisgeier/statsgov20gender.htm.

For every 100 girls diagnosed with a speech impairment 147 boys are similarly diagnosed. http://www.iteachilearn.com/uh/meisgeier/statsgov20gender.htm.

For every 100 girls diagnosed with mental retardation 138 boys are diagnosed as mentally retarded. http://www.iteachilearn.com/uh/meisgeier/statsgov20gender.htm.

For every 100 girls diagnosed with visual impairment 125 boys are visually impaired. http://www.iteachilearn.com/uh/meisgeier/statsgov20gender.htm.

For every 100 girls diagnosed with hearing impairment 108 boys are diagnosed as hearing impaired. http://www.iteachilearn.com/uh/ meisgeier/statsgov20gender.htm.

For every 100 girls diagnosed with deafness 120 boys have deafness. http://www.iteachilearn.com/uh/meisgeier/statsgov20gender.htm.

For every 100 girls with multiple disabilities 189 boys have multiple disabilities. http://www.iteachilearn.com/uh/meisgeier/statsgov 20gender.htm.

Source: Mortenson, Tom. 2006. "For Every 100 Girls . . ." Postsecondary.org. http://www.postsecondary.org/ archives/previous/ForEvery100Girls.pdf.

Appendix C

Home Writing Survey

Your name: _____ Date: _____

1. How often do you write at home?
   A. Often   B. Sometimes   C. Almost never

2. If so, where and when do you usually write?

3. What kinds of things do you write about at home? (poems, stories, raps, plays, etc.)

4. Do you ever "buddy-write" (collaborate with a friend) at home?

5. Mark which of these writing activities you do, if any, and estimate roughly how many minutes per day you spend on each.

   *Instant Messaging   _____   minutes: _____
   *Email   _____   minutes: _____
   *Writing on a blog
   or working on a website   _____   minutes: _____

6. Do you have your own website? (If so, tell me about it.)

7. I'd be interested in any other information you'd like to share with me.

Interview Between Carol Wilcox and Kadeem Wilcox

Carol is an assistant principal and Kadeem is a fifth-grade student in Denver, Colorado.

CW: Do you enjoy writing?

KADEEM: No, it's boring.

CW: Complete this sentence: "For me, the most enjoyable part about writing is . . . ?

KADEEM: Nothing.

CW: Complete this sentence: "For me, the worst part of writing is . . . ?"

KADEEM: To pick up the pencil. You already know that you are getting stressed at writing.

CW: What do you get stressed about?

KADEEM: The whatchamacallit, that you have to write to? The prompts.

CW: Why do those make you stressed?

KADEEM: 'Cause you only get to write to those.

CW: Do you ever get to write anything else?

KADEEM: If you get finished. But I never get finished.

CW: What else?

KADEEM: Sticking to that thing.

CW: Why is that hard?

KADEEM: Because you can't write about anything else.

CW: How would you rate yourself as a writer: (1) not very good; (2) about average; (3) pretty good; (4) strong?

KADEEM: Pretty good. Even though I don't like it, I get good grades. I get Bs or Cs or sometimes maybe an A.

CW: What's your favorite genre to write: personal narrative, poetry, fiction, nonfiction?

KADEEM: Poetry. Sometimes fiction too.

CW: In school what do you like to write about most?

KADEEM: Me and Devin write Professor Pillow stories. We've written eleven episodes. We write them at school at recess.

CW: Can you remember other school writing experiences that have been enjoyable?

KADEEM: Publishing a book I wrote. I wrote "Family Traditions" in fifth grade. I wrote it with the whole class. I wrote it in fifth grade. It still is getting published.

CW: Can you remember any painful writing experiences in school? Have you ever had to write for punishment?

KADEEM: Yes. Write sentences when I lied. And I had to do a refocus form about going to the bathroom at school when I wasn't supposed to.

CW: Do you write at home?

KADEEM: No, besides thank-you notes.

CW: Can you remember a time a teacher praised your writing?

KADEEM: It was in fourth grade. I even showed you. I went to your office. It was about planets. I was the first one done. They put all their words in the wrong place in the wrong order. They wrote messy, all scribbled dark and with smears. And I didn't have to erase once. I put my words really perfect. I wrote really neat.

CW: Can you remember a time a teacher steered you away from writing about something you wanted to write, or prevented you from writing about it?

KADEEM: No, but I heard her talking to another kid about it. She was talking to Gerson. He was going to write about the war. She told him he can't write about it because there was too much blood and violence and stuff.

CW: When it comes to writing, what do you consider the hardest part: (1) finding a good idea; (2) writing a first draft; (3) revising; (4) editing and correcting?

KADEEM: (*thinking hard*) Well, editing is hard. First you have to cross out all your mistakes and you don't know if your whole thing is a mistake and you might have to cross out your whole thing and start over again. You have to do your sloppy copy and then do it again. The whole class might be finished and you might not be.

CW: How would you rate your handwriting: (1) poor; (2) messy; (3) about average; (4) good?

KADEEM: Good.

CW: Please complete this sentence: When we write in school, I wish we were allowed to . . .

KADEEM: Write regular. Use whatever kind of words we wanted to in an argument, like words you can use outside of school.

The Follower

by Jack Gantos
from *Guys Write for Guys Read* edited by Jon Scieszka

My mother said he was trouble the first time I met him. His name was Frankie Pagoda and he had just been catapulted across the yard like a human cannonball and landed badly in ours. He was moaning as I stood over him, not knowing what to do. He was on his back and at first he wasn't moving, but slowly he began to gyrate his arms and legs like a stunned crab.

"Who are you?" I asked.

"Frankie . . . P—" he slowly replied. "Frankie Pagoda."

He was in a lot of pain, and here's what was going on. His older brother, Scary Gary, who had already been in trouble with the law, had made him climb to the very top of a reedy Australian pine tree with a rope between his teeth. Then he tied the rope to the top of the tree and Gary tied the other end to the winch on Mr. Pagoda's tow truck. He winched the tip of the tree all the way down so it made a big spring and then Frankie held on like a Koala bear while Gary cut the rope with a machete. Frankie was launched like the stones the Romans flung at the Vandals.

I was in my bedroom and Mom was in the kitchen; both of us had windows that faced the backyard. Then we heard that first *Whoosh!* of the tree and Frankie hollering, "*Ahhhhhhh!*" That was followed by a loud thud and a very soulful moan. And this is how we found him—on his back with his arms and legs slowly stretching out.

"Are you okay?" I asked. He slowly turned over onto his hands and knees.

"Yeah," he said, wincing. "I've had worse."

Mom pointed at him as if he were a garden pest. "He's a heap of trouble," she said to me. Then she said to Frankie, "If you have to hurt yourself, please do it in your own yard."

He seemed to nod to that and I helped him up and he ran off. A few minutes later we heard, "*Whoosh!*" Thud! "*Ugh!*" He was back.

"Something is messed up with those people," Mom said, chopping up onions that evening. "Something's wrong in their heads."

Maybe there was something wrong with me, too. I was different from Frankie but still, the first moment I saw him in pain, it occurred to me that I wanted to be in pain, too.

That evening my mother came into my room. "If I ever catch you playing with that kid or over at their house, you will be in big trouble. This is just a friendly warning," she said.

"Why?" I asked. "He's a neighbor and will probably be my friend."

"You should not be friends with kids who are a danger to themselves and others."

I got some courage up and replied, "That's what I love about him."

She pointed a red finger at my chest. "You are a follower, not a leader," she said bluntly. "You are putty in the wrong hands. Don't get me wrong. You're a nice kid, but you are most definitely a follower."

I sort of knew this was true but I didn't want to admit it to her. Plus, a little of me still wanted to believe that I was strong, that I was my own man and a great leader.

But within a week I was Frankie's man, which was pretty scary because he was Gary's man, which made me low man on the totem pole—or pine tree. The first time Gary launched me, I hit a car. It was an old Mercury Cougar parked in their backyard. It didn't have any wheels and sat on its belly like a cat crouching to catch a bird. I hit the roof, which was like a steel trampoline. It dented down and popped up and I went springing off the top. As I was in the air, I kept thinking, When you hit the ground, roll and tumble and it won't hurt so much. This is what I had learned from watching *Roller Derby* on TV. It was my favorite show and very violent, but the players always avoided massive debilitating and life-threatening injuries as long as they rolled and tumbled across the wooden track or over the rails and onto the rows of metal folding chairs. So, as I flew through the air, I stared at the grassy yard and planned my clever descent. I hit the ground with my outstretched arms and, instead of bouncing as if my hands were shock absorbers, I collapsed into the group like a piece of space junk.

I dislocated the fingers on my right hand, bruised the side of my face, and sprained my right shoulder. I limped home hunched over like Quasimodo and went straight to my room. A few minutes later I was barking in pain from relocating the joints in my fingers. I was so afraid my mother would see my bruised face that I stole my sister's makeup and powdered my bruise. At dinner I couldn't use my right arm. It hung limply by my side like an elephant's trunk. I must have pinched a nerve on contact with the ground that left my arm paralyzed. Perhaps for life. I ate with my left hand and food kept falling down my chin and shirt and onto my lap.

"What's wrong with your arm?" my mother asked.

"Nothing," I mumbled.

She sneered, stood up, and came around to my side. She grabbed my arm and pulled on it like it was the starter rope on a lawnmower engine. Something deep inside my shoulder went *Pop!*

"Arghhh," I sighed. The relief from the pain was heavenly.

"You are dumb as a post," my mother said. "I'm warning you— don't play with that kid! He'll lead you to your death."

I couldn't help myself. The next day I felt pretty good and my teeth no longer throbbed when I breathed through my mouth. As soon as my mother went into the bathroom I ran over to Frankie's house. His brother Gary had rigged up an electric chair with a train transformer. He ran copper leads from the transformer to chicken wire on the chair and duct-taped it down.

"Don't be a chicken," he said demonically when he saw me. "Take a seat."

I did and it was torture at its most challenging. When I got home I looked at my naked butt in the mirror, and it was singed with the same chicken wire pattern that was on the chair. "Wow," I said. "Pretty cool."

The next day my mother did the laundry. She came to me with my pants, which were singed with the same wire pattern. "You don't have to tell me how this happened," she said. "You just have to stop. Whatever drives you to do this stuff is a sickness. So I'm grounding you for a while until you start displaying some sense."

Maybe I was sick. Maybe I was a follower. But I couldn't help myself. I wanted to sneak back for more. I was just thinking of crawling out the window when I looked over at the Pagoda house, and Frankie had his bike up on the peak of his roof. He was poised to pedal down the slope and land in the pool, which was quite a distance from the eaves of the house.

"Go!" Gary demanded. Frankie did. He pedaled as far as he could and yelled all the way down and then was in the air. My vision was blocked by a bush, and instead of a splashing sound there was the springy metal sound of his bike hitting the concrete patio and clattering around. In a minute Gary was hollering at him to stop being a sissy and to get up and the dent in his forehead wasn't anything to cry over. I rubbed my hand over my forehead. *Perhaps a little dent in my own would look good*, I thought.

The ambulance arrived in a few minutes. After some begging, Mom allowed me to visit Frankie in the hospital, and later, once Scary Gary was sent off to a special program for dangerous boys, I even snuck over to Frankie's house a few times. He recovered just fine. And because he stopped doing dumb things for Gary, I stopped doing dumb things for him. He was a follower too, like me. And when you put two followers together nothing really bad happens. We didn't get hurt for a while or do anything too stupid. About a month went by before I secretly hoped Scary Gary would return home and rescue us from being so dull. I was bored out of my mind.

References

Allen, Jennifer. 2006. *Becoming a Literacy Leader: Supporting Learning and Change.* Portland, ME: Stenhouse.

American Association of University Women Educational Foundation. 1992. *How Schools Shortchange Girls: A Study of Major Findings on Girls and Education.* New York: Marlowe and Company.

Anderson, Carl. 2005. *Assessing Writers.* Portsmouth, NH: Heinemann.

———. 2000. *How's It Going? A Practical Guide to Conferring with Student Writers.* Portsmouth, NH: Heinemann.

Barbieri, Maureen. 1995. *Sounds from the Heart: Learning to Listen to Girls.* Portsmouth, NH: Heinemann.

Barry, Dave. 1997. *Dave Barry Slept Here: A Sort of History of the U.S.* New York: Ballantine Books.

Booth, David. 2000. *Even Hockey Players Read.* Portland, ME: Stenhouse.

Brand, Max. 2004. *Word Savvy: Integrating Vocabulary, Spelling, and Word Study.* Portland, ME: Stenhouse.

Brand, Max, and Gayle Brand. 2006. *Practical Fluency: Classroom Perspectives, Grades K–6.* Portland, ME: Stenhouse.

Britton, James. 1970. *Language and Learning.* Harmondsworth, UK: Penguin.

Connell, Diane, and Betsy Gunzelmann. 2004. "The New Gender Gap." *Instructor.* March. Available online at http://teacher. scholastic.com/products/ Instructor/Mar04_gendergap.htm.

Csikszentmihalyi, Mihaly. 1991. *Flow: The Psychology of Optimal Experience.* New York: HarperCollins.

Dyson, Ann Haas. 1993. *Social Worlds of Children Learning to Write in an Urban Primary School.* New York: T. C. Press.

Essoyan, Pamela. 2006. "The Boy Brain: Wired to Go." *Honolulu Star-Bulletin.* May 28.

Farris, Pamela. 1991. *Language Arts.* Urbana, IL: National Council of Teachers of English.

Fay, Kathleen, and Suzanne Whaley. 2004. *Becoming One Community: Reading and Writing with English Language Learners.* Portland, ME: Stenhouse.

Fletcher, Ralph. 1993. *What a Writer Needs.* Portsmouth, NH: Heinemann.

Fletcher, Ralph, and JoAnn Portalupi. 2002. *When Students Write.* DVD and VHS. Portland, ME: Stenhouse.

Geirland, John. 1996. "Go with the Flow." *Wired* (September). Available online at http://www.wired.com/wired/archive/4.09/czik.html.

Gurian, Michael. 2005a. "Disappearing Act." *The Washington Post.* December 4: B1.

———. 2005b. *The Minds of Boys: Saving Our Sons from Falling Behind in School and Life.* New York: Jossey-Bass.

Harman, Claire. 2005a. *Myself and the Other Fellow: A Life of Robert Louis Stevenson.* New York: HarperCollins.

———. 2005b. "Robert Louis Stevenson's Split Personality." Interview on *Weekend Edition Sunday.* National Public Radio. November 27.

Harwayne, Shelley. 1999. *Going Public: Priorities and Practice at the Manhattan New School.* Portsmouth, NH: Heinemann.

Johnston, Peter H. 2004. *Choice Words: How Our Language Affects Children's Learning.* Portland, ME: Stenhouse.

Kaufman, Douglas. 2000. *Conferences and Conversations: Listening to the Literate Classroom.* Portsmouth, NH: Heinemann.

Kindlon, Dan, and Michael Thompson. 2000. *Raising Cain: Protecting the Emotional Life of Boys.* New York: Ballantine Books.

Kleinfeld, Judith. 1998. "The Myth That Schools Shortchange Girls: Social Science in the Service of Deception." http://www.uaf.edu/ northern/ schools/download.html.

Lane, Barry. 2003. *Fifty-One Wacky We-Search Reports*. Shoreham, VT: Discover Writing Press.

Lewin, Tamar. 2006. "Boys Are No Match for Girls in Completing High School." *The New York Times*. April 19.

McCauley, Mary Beth. 2005. "Matching Boys with Books." *Christian Science Monitor*. May 24.

Morgan, Bruce. 2005. *Writing Through the Tween Years: Supporting Writers, Grades 3–6*. Portland, ME: Stenhouse.

Mortenson, Tom. 2006. "For Every 100 Girls . . ." *Postsecondary Education OPPORTUNITY*. April 26. http://www.postsecondary. org/archives/previous/ForEvery100Girls.pdf.

Newkirk, Thomas. 2002. *Misreading Masculinity: Boys, Literacy, and Popular Culture*. Portsmouth, NH: Heinemann.

Parker, Emelie, and Tess Pardini. 2006. *"The Words Came Down!" English Language Learners Read, Write, and Talk Across the Curriculum, K–2*. Portland, ME: Stenhouse.

Peterson, Shelley. 2000. "Fourth, Sixth, and Eighth Graders Preferred Writing Topics and Identification of Gender Markers in Stories." *Elementary School Journal* 101: 79–100.

Pollack, William. 1998. *Real Boys: Rescuing Our Sons from the Myths of Boyhood*. New York: Random House.

Power, Brenda Miller. 1995. "Bearing Walls and Writing Workshops." *Language Arts* 72 (November): 482–488.

Rief, Linda. 2003. *One Hundred Quickwrites: Fast and Effective Freewriting Exercises That Build Students' Confidence, Develop Their Fluency, and Bring Out the Writer in Every Student*. New York: Scholastic.

———. 2006. "What's Right with Writing." *Voices from the Middle*. 13 (4): 32–39.

Sax, Leonard. 2005. *Why Gender Matters: What Parents and Teachers Need to Know About the Emerging Science of Sex Differences*. New York: Doubleday.

Short, Kathy G., Jerome C. Harste, and Carolyn Burke. 1995. *Creating Classrooms for Authors and Inquirers*. Portsmouth, NH: Heinemann.

Silverman, Linda. 2002. *Upside-Down Brilliance: The Visual-Spatial Learner.* Glendale, CO: Deleon.

————. 2003. "Poor Handwriting: A Major Cause of Underachievement." Visual-Spatial Resource. http://www.visualspatial.org/ Articles/poorhand.pdf.

Smith, Michael W., and Jeffrey G. Wilhelm. 2002. *Reading Don't Fix No Chevys: Literacy in the Lives of Young Men.* Portsmouth, NH: Heinemann.

Sommers, Christina Hoff. 2001. *The War Against Boys: How Misguided Feminism Is Harming Our Young Men.* New York: Simon and Schuster.

————. 2004. "The Write Stuff." *Education Reporter.* January.

Szymusiak, Karen, and Franki Sibberson. 2001. *Beyond Leveled Books: Supporting Transitional Readers in Grades 2–5.* Portland, ME: Stenhouse.

Tannen, Deborah. 2001. *You Just Don't Understand: Women and Men in Conversation.* New York: HarperCollins.

Toye, Sue. 2000. "Boys' Writing Perceived Worse Than Girls." University of Toronto. Oct. 18. http://www.news.utoronto.ca/bin1/001018c.asp.

Tyre, Peg. 2006. "The Trouble with Boys." *Newsweek.* January 30.

U.S. Department of Education. 2003. Institute of Education Sciences. National Center for Education Statistics. *The Nation's Report Card: Writing 2002,* NCES 2003-529, by H. R. Persky, M. C. Daane, and Y. Jin. Washington, D.C.

Wells, Cyrene. 1996. *Literacies Lost: When Students Move from a Progressive Middle School to a Traditional High School.* New York: Teachers College Press.

Children's Literature Cited

Creech, Sharon. 2001. *Love That Dog.* New York: Joanna Cotler.

Fletcher, Ralph. 1998. *Flying Solo.* New York: Clarion Books.

————. 2002. *Uncle Daddy.* New York: Henry Holt.

————. 2004. *Hello Harvest Moon.* New York: Clarion Books.

————. 2005. *Marshfield Dreams: When I Was a Kid.* New York: Henry Holt.

Gall, Chris. 2006. *Dear Fish.* New York: Little, Brown.

Griffiths, Andy. 2004. *Zombie Butts from Uranus!* New York: Scholastic.

Hoey, Edwin A. 1994. "Foul Shot." In *On Common Ground*, ed. Jerry George, Don Stone, and Faye Ward. Don Mills, ON: Oxford University Press Canada.

Moss, Marissa. 2003. *Max's Logbook.* New York: Scholastic.

Paulsen, Gary. 1995. *Harris and Me.* New York: Dell Yearling.

Pilkey, Dav. 2006. *Captain Underpants and the Preposterous Plight of the Purple Potty People.* New York: The Blue Sky Press.

Pilkey, Dav. 1998. *Dumb Bunnies.* New York: The Blue Sky Press.

Shannon, David. 1998. *No, David!* New York: The Blue Sky Press.

Scieszka, Jon. 2005. *Guys Write for Guys Read.* New York: Viking Penguin.

Spier, Peter. 1994. *The Fox Went Out on a Chilly Night: An Old Song.* New York: Dell.

Spinelli, Jerry. 1998. *Knots in My Yo-yo String: The Autobiography of a Kid.* New York: Knopf.

Wiesner, David. 1997. *Tuesday.* New York: Clarion Books.

Index